# Foundations

## Spiritual Formation

Center for Biblical Leadership

White Wing Publishing House

Cleveland, TN USA and Other Countries

ACD—1997

Foundations–Spiritual Formation
Copyright ©1997
Published by White Wing Publishing House
P. O. Box 3000
Cleveland, TN 37320-3000
(423) 559-5425 • 1-800-221-5027
All rights reserved
Cover Illustration: Perry Horner
First Published, 1997; Eleventh Printing 2009

ISBN 978-1-889505-10-7

# Preface

This Foundations Course (Spiritual Formation) by the Center for Biblical Leadership is presented with the hope that it will provide a basic knowledge of the principles to be embraced by those who are committed to Jesus Christ. We acknowledge freely His headship of the Church He is building and we are dedicated to follow Him faithfully.

Being rather broad in scope, there is not an attempt to deal with many of the specifics which subsequently it will be necessary to explore more fully. It will be revised and updated from time to time to assure current relevance to the needs of our people.

We sincerely appreciate all the research and work that has been done in the preparation of this foundations course. It is presented as a foundational tool with the prayer that it will contribute to a more knowledgeable and a more competent leadership for God's people.

This course could be valuable locally for group or individual study. May God's grace add richness to what we are presenting here which will make our thrust into the harvest more effective.

BILLY D. MURRAY
General Overseer
1990–2000

# INTRODUCTION

This course of study is an important contribution to the ongoing process of leadership development and discipleship in the Church of God of Prophecy. It is designed for study by anyone who desires to increase their understanding of the biblical principles of spiritual growth and personal spiritual maturity. It should be of special interest to those preparing for the ministry. The course may be studied individually of by local congregations seeking resources for Christian education programs.

A variety of sources are cited throughout the course, and may be referred to by the student for further study. These are not the only sources where more in-depth information may be found, but they are suitable as introductory texts.

At the end of this booklet is a self-administered examination that will demonstrate the student's grasp of the study material. A more extensive examination is required for ministerial candidates, and is administered by the state or national review board.

Below is the goal and objectives established for this course.

## Spiritual Formation

Goal: The individual will demonstrate an understanding of the processes of spiritual formation.

Unit One—The individual will demonstrate an understanding of the processes of spiritual formation through the influences of:
    a.  Transformation
    b.  Experiencing God
    c.  Societal Influences
    d.  Spiritual Exercise
    e.  Motivation
    f.  Call to Holiness
    g.  History of Seekers
    h.  Abundant Life

i.  Holiness of God
j.  Celebration
k.  The Body
l.  Temptation
m.  Condemnation
n.  Humility
o.  Brokenness
p.  Communion
q.  Walking in the Spirit
r.  Love
s.  Evangelism
t.  Equipping
u.  Gifts of Grace
v.  Community
w.  Faith
x.  Spiritual Warfare

Unit Two — The individual will demonstrate an understanding of the processes of spiritual formation through understanding the spiritual disciplines:
a.  Prayer
b.  Fasting
c.  Meditation
d.  Study
e.  Journaling
f.  Confession
g.  Solitude
h.  Service

It is the purpose of this course of study that the individual will find it useful in the development of his/her understanding of God's truth and purposes. In the final analysis it is one's application of this knowledge through prayer and a vital relationship with Christ that makes it valuable. Proverbs 2:1-7 says, "My son, if thou wilt receive my words, and hide my commandments with thee; So that thou incline thine ear unto wisdom, and apply thine heart to understanding; Yea, if thou criest after knowledge, and liftest up thy voice for understanding; If thou seekest her as silver, and searchest for her as for hid treasures; Then shalt thou understand the fear of the LORD, and find the knowledge of God. For the LORD giveth wisdom: out of his mouth cometh knowledge and understanding. He layeth up sound wisdom for the righteous: he is a buckler to them that walk uprightly."

# CONTENTS

# INSTRUCTIONS

This course of study is designed to be used by an individual who wants to further his or her understanding of the foundations of the faith, one who is in the process of obtaining ministerial credentials, or a local church who wants to use it as a study course. The examination, found in the back of the book, has been developed to demonstrate one's knowledge of the objective. It has been written to be a self-administered, open-book examination. If the registration form, which is included in the back of the book, is used, one (1) Leadership Development Unit (LDU) may be earned for the completion of this course.

**Individual Study** *(NOT a minister, ministerial candidate, or candidate for Certified Teacher)*

This course of study may be taken as an individual study by anyone who desires to improve his/her understanding of the Bible. In this case, the individual will be responsible to read the assigned materials and take the examination at his or her own pace. You may earn one (1) Leadership Development Unit for the completion of this course. To earn this credit, please fill out form in back of book and send with your exam to the state/regional/national office for grading. A certificate of completion will be granted by the state/regional/national office and appropriate records kept.

**Individual Study** *(Ministers, ministerial candidates, or candidates for Certified Teacher)*

A minister, ministerial candidate, or candidate for the Certified Teacher Certificate may earn one (1) Leadership Development Unit for the completion of this course. To earn this credit, the individual will need to register for this course of study with the state/regional/national office (registration form is included with examination in the back of the book). Once the course of study has been completed, the examination should be reviewed by the person's pastor and submitted to the state/regional/national office. A Certificate of Completion will be granted by the state/regional/national office and appropriate records kept. The overseer and Ministerial Review Board may exempt an applicant from this course if significant knowledge can be validated through other equivalent educational programs.

## Group Courses

Persons who take this course in an approved group study will receive a Certificate of Completion to validate the completion of the requirements. Such group studies will be conducted by the Pastor or an instructor approved by the Pastor. The instructor will be responsible for teaching the course, giving and grading exams, and sending the completed Examination Report Form to the Center for Biblical Leadership at the International Offices. The instructor will find the answer keys and Examination Report Form in the instructor's packet which was provided at purchase for those taking a group study.

In order for those participating in a study course to be granted a Certificate of Completion, the following requirements must be met:

1) The instructor must be the Pastor or approved by the Pastor.
2) The course must consist of at least ten hours of instruction, and the student must not have more than two hours of valid absences.
3) The student must read the text and successfully complete the examination which accompanies the text.

# Spiritual Formation

**GOAL: THE INDIVIDUAL WILL DEMONSTRATE AN UNDERSTANDING OF THE PROCESSES OF SPIRITUAL FORMATION.**

Spiritual formation is the process of shaping and growth in the life of a Christian toward the goal of being conformed to the image of Christ. Two influences impact the formation of every believer: God's grace and man's response. Through many approaches God seeks to call man into His presence and to mold man into His image. At times there are moments of crisis where believers are drawn dramatically to life transformation. These are of great value. For the remainder of the time spiritual formation comes as an almost imperceptible process intertwined with daily experience. As believers understand the influences at work and the approaches of God, they can be more responsive for positive spiritual formation. In addition, as believers learn how they can participate with God through spiritual disciplines, their experiences and formation will be greatly enhanced.

For leaders and believers called to specific ministries, understanding and participation for spiritual formation is vital. Ministry of eternal value cannot be accomplished without God's leadership. As time and ministry advance in these last days, God will be using men and women who are intimately in tune with Him personally. He will need to lead in regions and in ways that may be unfamiliar. Only ministers made sensitive to God through lives of close communion will be able to respond to His unique last-days prompting. This sensitivity will come from lives fully given over to seeking Him and spending time with Him, those who have been formed by Him.

This material is designed to provide the individual with foundational knowledge of the process of spiritual formation. This will be done by introducing the individual to important topics dealing with the approaches of God and man's responses. At the beginning of each specific section an objective will be given to guide the learning process.

The last section of this material is a self-administered examination that will be used to ensure that the individual will be able to meet the stated objectives. This exam will serve to reinforce the learning of significant and necessary material. The individual should look at this exam with the purpose of learning the expected objectives.

May we join together on this most glorious and noble journey of walking with God.

# Spiritual Formation Through Influences

## Unit One

# Objective:

The individual will demonstrate an understanding of the process of spiritual formation through various *influences.*

### Influences:

| | | |
|---|---|---|
| Transformation | Holiness of God | Walking in the Spirit |
| Experiencing God | Celebration | Love |
| Societal Influences | Body | Evangelism |
| Spiritual Exercise | Temptation | Equipping |
| Motivation | Condemnation | Gifts of Grace |
| Call to Holiness | Humility | Community |
| History | Brokenness | Spiritual Warfare |
| Abundant New Life | Communion | Faith |

## TRANSFORMATION

**Objective:** The individual will demonstrate an understanding of the processes of spiritual formation through *transformation* by identifying Bible figures whose lives demonstrate this quality.

> "Therefore if any man be in Christ, he is a new creature: old things are passed away; behold, all things are become new" (2 Corinthians 5:17).

Apart from a radically new principle of life, humanity simply cannot advance far. It is only the real presence of Christ in His mature people interspersed throughout the 'secular' life that will cause the necessary [reform]. . . .The real presence of Christ as a governing force will come solely as His called out people occupy their stations in the holiness and power characteristic of Him, as they demonstrate to the world the way to live that is best in every respect.[1]

---

**Principle:** *People with receptive hearts are transformed in the presence of Christ.*

---

Transformation is the goal for which God has destined all those who will believe on Him. He tells us in Romans 12:2 not to be conformed to this world, but to be transformed by the renewing of our minds.

Transformation is a part of the redeeming act at salvation; we are regenerated, made new. Yet transformation is also a process by which Christ is shaping believers into His likeness, conforming us to His image. This is not a crisis experience, but a process of His grace working in us.

Transformation is illustrated by Isaiah's encounter with God as described in Isaiah 6. Notice he saw the Lord, and he experienced His glory. From that he was convicted, he was cleansed, and he was called. His life was touched, never to be the same, after having experienced the transforming presence of God.

This is also illustrated in Peter's life as described in Luke 5:1-11. At the revelation of Who Peter had met by the waterside, he responded in several ways. These are frequently characteristic of those who realize they are in the presence of the Lord:

| | |
|---|---|
| He fell | —his self-sufficiency melted |
| | —he was humbled |
| He confessed | —his self-righteousness melted |
| | —he was repentant |
| He was astonished | —his self-understanding melted |
| | —he believed |
| He responded | —his self-employment melted |
| | —he was called |

From these illustrations we can see some common threads of transformation:

1. God must reveal Himself to man. Man cannot find God or search Him out to understand or know Him. God, through revelation, brings man to the divine encounter.

2. This experience in God's presence is always God-centered. It is not man-centered with God as one of several actors. He is the center, transcending all, around which everything else is formed and transformed.
3. Because of the nature of God, any meeting with man cannot be self-centered. This is contrary to human nature and demonstrates the miracle of transformation.
4. In God's transforming presence there is dialogue. God reveals, man responds.

> **Principle:** *Transformation can be experienced gradually as well as instantaneously. It is a never-ending process where the believer is being conformed to the image of Christ.*

"But we all, with open face beholding as in a glass the glory of the Lord, are changed into the same image from glory to glory, even as by the Spirit of the Lord" (2 Corinthians 3:18; see also Romans 8:29; 12:1-2; Galatians 4:19; Colossians 3:10).

Here the transformation is described as metamorphosis. We know this as the slow-changing process of growth in plants. It is empowered through exposure to the sun. Similarly we, as believers, are engaged in the continuous ongoing process of growth which is empowered by exposure to Christ.

*Dallas Willard,* The Spirit of the Disciplines, *p. 70.*

The approach to wholeness is for humankind a process of great length and difficulty that engages all our own powers to their fullest extent over a long course of experience. But we don't like to hear this. We are somewhat misled by the reports of experiences by many great spiritual leaders, and we assign their greatness to these great moments they were given, neglecting the years of slow progress they endured before them. Francis de Sales wisely counsels us not to expect transformation in a moment, though it is possible for God to give it.

The ordinary purification and healing, whether of the body or of the mind, takes place only little by little, by passing from one degree to another with patience. The angels upon Jacob's ladder had wings; yet they flew not, but ascended and descended in order from one step to another. The soul that rises from sin to devotion may be compared to the dawning of the day, which at its approach does not expel the darkness instantaneously but only little by little.[2]

Thus, it is necessary to say that crisis conversion, as understood in Christian circles, is not the same thing as *the required transformation of the self.* The fact that a long course of experience is needed for the transformation is not set aside when we are touched by the new life from above. Some well-known scenes from the life of one of Jesus' closest friends, Simon Peter, the "rock," who, upon occasion, more resembled the pile of shifting sand, illustrates this fact well.

> **Key:** *Transformation naturally takes place, whether as a crisis, or gradually, or both, through exposure to the revelation of the presence of Christ.*

## EXPERIENCING GOD

**Objective:** The individual will demonstrate an understanding of the processes of spiritual formation through *experiencing God* by contrasting simple knowledge of God with knowing God relationally.

Our Knowledge of God rests on the revelation of His personal presence. . . Of such a presence it must be true that to those who have never been confronted with it argument is useless, while to those who have, it is superfluous.[3]

*Yada* is the Hebrew word for "to know," used often in the Old Testament. In the New Testament, the Greek word *ginoskein* carries similar meaning from the Hebrew understanding and use of *yada* because the New Testament writers wrote from the foundation of their Jewish backgrounds where *yada* was prevalent.

This is a word which refers to knowing more by the heart than through the mind, knowing not from objective observation but from active and intentional engagement in lived experience. Knowledge in the Hebrew mind is not thought of as a possession of information. It is rather knowledge for its exercise or actualization.[4]

Knowing in the Hebrew mind was more relational, experiential, and engaging. The modern Greek mind of the New Testament day had shifted to see knowledge as being objective, detached, and rational. With the coming of Christ and the gospel it was the personal, relational knowing of the Hebrew *yada* that most effectively conveyed His truth.

Christ was a Person, the Son of God, to be known and trusted intimately. He was not simply propositional truth or factual documentation. He called for personal response in life commitment far beyond intellectual assent. To know Him, believers must experience Him (*yada*). No one can know Christ because they have studied Him or observed Him (Greek mind); He must be believed, trusted, obeyed, received, or in a word — experienced in a personal way (*yada*).

## Jesus

In John 17:3 Jesus calls for believers to experience Him, "And this is life eternal, that they might know thee the only true God, and Jesus Christ, whom thou hast sent." This knowing is not just mental assent but the deep relational knowing of communion with Christ. Jesus was not implying that His disciples have mere acquaintance knowledge; He wanted them to experience a rich relationship with God for a life of ministry and fulfillment.

## Paul

Paul requests in Philippians 3:10, "That I may know him, and the power of his resurrection, and the fellowship of his sufferings, being made conformable unto his death." This verse of Scripture shows the high call to experience God. If anyone had experienced God, surely it was Paul, the greatest missionary evangelist of the New Testament. Yet at the end of his ministry he is still seeking to "know" (experience) more of God. Paul realized there would always be more of God to discover. This will be the unfolding revelation of eternity.

## Moses

Moses challenges in Exodus 33:13, "Now therefore, I pray thee, if I have found grace in thy sight, show me now thy way, that I may know thee, that I may find grace in thy sight. . . ." Moses, in this chapter, shows a heart that is intent on experiencing God intimately. He hears God and is directed by an angel, God appears in the pillar of cloud, God speaks to him face to face, yet Moses still presses for further encounter, to see God's glory! Moses demonstrates a driving passion to know God deeply.

The word *yada* is used in the Old Testament for intimate friendship. The love between Jonathan and David illustrates this. Also, covenant relations which bound men and families together, or even the intimacy of the act of lovemaking, are described in the Old Testament by the word *Yada*. Shallow knowing, limited to information or factual content, does not approach the engagement or commitment of these Old Testament uses. This is how Christ seeks to be "known" by His followers.

Another illustration is the comparison between newlyweds knowing one another and the senior couple who has been married for over fifty years. The former know one another well enough to be married, while the latter have a knowledge of one another that has been developed by the years of experience together. Again, this is how Christ seeks to be known by His followers.

Knowing God "becomes seeking God, not knowledge, fullness, not facts, a first-hand encounter where meeting Him is better than a secondhand testimony of Him. Let God become as real and full to us as the world was when we were sinners. In sin the world was not studied to learn sin. It was experienced through activity and involvement. One engages in sin to know it. One could never say they know sin by reading about it. They have not known its vicelike grip or destructive cravings. Neither should one say they have known God from a simple mental assent to His existence and some attendance to religious gatherings."[5]

## SOCIETAL INFLUENCES

**Objective:** The individual will demonstrate an understanding of the processes of spiritual formation in *societal influences* by discussing such influences and their impact on believers.

Christianity has not so much been tried and found wanting, as it has been found difficult and left untried.
— G. K. Chesterton

> **Key:** *Deformed life is never as attractive or empowering as real life.*

"And be not conformed to this world: but be ye transformed by the renewing of your mind, that ye may prove what is that good, and acceptable, and perfect, will of God" (Romans 12:2).

## DILEMMA

The only cure for the human condition is a spiritual one. In December, 1992, an article was written in the Wall Street Journal on inner city problems and their solutions. Amazingly, the writer concluded that there would be no cure for the inner cities regardless of the money poured into the despicable situations, until there was aid for the spiritual demise of the people found there.

Yet modern Christianity is seen as powerless, archaic, and irrelevant. There is little practical, tangible difference between the world and believers according to polls taken over the last decade.[6] Though one insightful reporter may have seen the spiritual need, the secularizing trend in society has ostracized Christianity as outmoded and out of touch with modern reality. *Ministries committed to spiritual formation and growth are challenged in this age to articulate their stand for what is seen as ineffective and unfounded faith.*

## COUNTER TRENDS

**Materialism:** The theory that physical matter is the only reality and that everything, including thought, feeling, mind, and will, can be explained in terms of matter; the theory that worldy possessions constitute the highest value in life. Society values things above people. Because of this, people are devalued and used to get things rather than the converse, things used to benefit people. The mentality is spread heavily through mass media and entertainment since it fuels the profits of corporate America.

**Caution:** Materialism is one of the deadliest threats to faith in industrialized nations. Believers continue with their forms of worship while the idol of mammon ascends. The subtle influence of this philosophy fills every part of life, especially one's identity. People are judged, not by character quality, but by what they possess.

**Humanism:** The philosophy that places man in the center of his universe. This is contrary to biblical faith since God is the center of all that He has made. In reality, humanism dethrones God and establishes man's place of preeminence in society. There, man is deified by the faith that the innate goodness of man can achieve peace and world harmony.

**Caution:** The Bible teaches not the innate goodness of man, but the fallen nature of man needing a Savior. Man apart from God will only duplicate Babel.

**Pluralism:** The belief that there are many ways to truth. This opens the door for the fall of absolutes. Each person is free to choose his own path without discrimination, and seemingly without regard for his effect on the society as a whole. This throws morality as defined by past standards out the window.

**Caution:** All philosophies are accepted, with the exception of Christianity, since it proclaims one truth, God's Word, and one Savior, Jesus Christ. Believers are seen as naive, ignorant, and bigoted since they will not accept many ways and many gods.

**Spiritualism:** Renewed openness to the unseen realm. The door is swinging wide for society to renew an age-old dance with spiritists, the occult, and mystics. The answer to the problems of mankind have not been found in science or industry. Now the spiritual realm becomes the next frontier to utopia.

**Caution:** Satan is tempting the world to go deeper from the truth and into his darkness. Yet this is a great time for believers to proclaim that they know the personal Spirit of the universe, God the Father. Receptivity to the miraculous is very high.

**Disconnected Faith:** Mental assent without accompanying obedience or transformation. To some, faith is seen as a purely inward thing producing no effect until eternity and heaven. Many believers attempt pure faith with little hope of pure life.

**Caution:** Here faith is disconnected from the responsibility to live right. Often believers think they cannot live above their sins, so there is no reason to try. They know they are forgiven. In this way Satan robs them of abundant life on earth.

**Superficial Living:** Focuses on forgiveness rather than on living. Faith does not impact ethical practices. There is a cross focus in contrast to the New Testament Church emphasis on the resurrection life. Belief and doctrines are exalted above life and practice.

**Caution:** People may be Christian while they are not committed disciples. Faith for the moment becomes prevalent, in place of faith as a trusting relationship in Christ.

**No Transformation:** Holiness seen as an ideal, not a real goal of spiritual life or practical living in the present. Many accept the feeling that holiness may be attained only beyond this life.

**Caution:** With this assumption comes the futility of ever attempting a life of holiness. If it is impossible and not expected till eternity, why trouble with it?

---

**Call:** *The age-old mandate of the Church must be activated in this generation.*

---

"Let your light so shine before men, that they may see your good works, and glorify your Father which is in heaven" (Matthew 5:16).

"That ye may be blameless and harmless, the sons of God, without rebuke, in the midst of a crooked and perverse nation, among whom ye shine as lights in the world" (Philippians 2:15).

## SPIRITUAL EXERCISE

**Objective:** The individual will demonstrate an understanding of the processes of spiritual formation with regard to *spiritual exercise,* by describing how such exercise brings freedom.

"Know ye not that they which run in a race run all, but one receiveth the prize? So run, that ye may obtain. And every man that striveth for the mastery is temperate in all things. Now they do it to obtain a corruptible crown; but we an incorruptible. I therefore so run, not as uncertainly; so fight I, not as one that beateth the air: But I keep under my body, and bring it into subjection: lest that by any means, when I have preached to others, I myself should be a castaway" (1 Corinthians 9:24-27).

"But refuse profane and old wives' fables, and exercise thyself rather unto godliness. For bodily exercise profiteth little: but godliness is profitable unto all things, having promise of the life that now is, and of that which is to come" (1 Timothy 4:7, 8).

The word "exercise" comes from the Greek *gymnasia,* meaning "training" or "exercise."[7] Note the similarity in the word *gymnasium.* It is also found in:

"But strong meat belongeth to them that are of full age, even those who by reason of use have their senses exercised to discern both good and evil" (Hebrews 5:14).

"Now no chastening for the present seemeth to be joyous, but grievous: nevertheless afterward it yieldeth the peaceable fruit of righteousness unto them which are exercised thereby" (Hebrews 12:1).

"Having eyes full of adultery, and that cannot cease from sin; beguiling unstable souls: an heart they have exercised with covetous practices; cursed children" (2 Peter 2:14).

It is illustrated by those who have distinguished themselves:

Mike Singletary, professional football middle linebacker, did not have the size of others at six feet two and possibly 220 pounds. He did not have exceptional speed. He did not have the natural gifts that allow others to excel in football, yet he was Defensive Player of the Year twice, often on the All Pro Team, and member of the Super Bowl XXV Dream Team. Mike credits the habitual discipline of preparing for games long after the other team mates had gone home.

Ernest Hemingway, well-known author, was a perfectionist when it came to his writing. "It is a well-known fact that he wrote the conclusion to his novel, *A Farewell To Arms,* seventeen times in an effort to get it right."[8] His economy of style was honed by hours of disciplined writing and rewriting, learning the art of language.

Leonardo da Vinci on one occasion drew a thousand hands in disciplined training for his art. Thomas Edison invented the incandescent light after years of failure and over one thousand attempts.

These men and many more testify to the freedom that comes through discipline. To watch a Chet Atkins or Roy Clark as they easily move their fingers over the guitar frets hides the fact that their artistry has been released through two lifetimes of practice. They have liberty on their instruments because they have spent the time in disciplined preparation.

Dr. Devries spent hours practicing heart surgery on pigs and other small animals before performing the first open heart surgery. He said he was practicing to act naturally.

Most Christians pray for the power to respond properly to temptation, but it is in the daily commitments to spiritual exercise that such power is developed. Believers can grow to act naturally as children of God. The life they experience in their times of daily discipline becomes their natural response to the pressures of Satan and testing.

Elton Trueblood wrote:

We have not advanced very far in our spiritual lives if we have not encountered the basic paradox of freedom . . . that we are most free when we are bound. But not just any way of being bound will suffice; what matters is the character of our binding. The one who would be an athlete, but who is unwilling to discipline his body by regular exercise and abstinence, is not free to excel on the field or the track. His failure to train rigorously denies him the freedom to run with the desired speed and endurance. With one united voice, the giants of the devotional life apply the same principle to the whole life: Discipline is the price of freedom.[9]

William Barclay said it powerfully: "Nothing was ever achieved without discipline." Many an athlete and many a man has been ruined because he abandoned discipline and let himself grow slack. Coleridge is the supreme tragedy of indiscipline. Never did so great a mind produce so little. He left Cambridge University to join the army; but he left the army because, in spite of all his erudition, he could not rub down a horse; he returned to Oxford and left without a degree. He began a paper called *The Watchman* which lived for ten numbers and then died. It has been said of him: "He lost himself in visions of work to be done, that always remained to be done. Coleridge had every poetic gift but one — the gift of sustained and concentrated effort." In his head and in his mind he had all kinds of books "completed save for transcription." But the books were never composed outside his mind. "No one ever reached any eminence, and no one having reached it ever maintained it, without discipline."[10]

## MOTIVATION

**Objective:** The individual will demonstrate an understanding of the processes of spiritual formation in *motivation* by identifying legalistic motives and proper motives.

The spiritual disciplines are intended for our good. They are meant to bring the abundance of God into our lives. It is possible, however, to turn them into another set of soul-killing laws. Law bound disciplines breathe death.[11]

> ***Principle:*** *We must avoid externalism, laws, and control over others while we make every attempt at cultivating or drawing near for God's work of inner transformation.*

*Legalism is superstition.* " 'Legalism' holds that overt action conforming to rules for explicit behavior is what makes us right and pleasing to God and worthy of blessing."[12] Jesus calls it the righteousness of the scribes and Pharisees (Matthew 5:20). It is interesting to note that the Pharisees were compelled by two types of motivation, pride or fear. If a person was a "good" Pharisee then he felt the pride of knowing he was among the best Jews of the nation. If he was a "not so good" Pharisee then he was motivated by the fear that he needed to improve to avoid exposure as a breaker of the law. Either motivation is far below the divine motive of love.

## ILLUSTRATIONS

A farmer has no power to produce grain, only God can do that. Still, the farmer wisely understands his role of placing the grain in the right environment for growth. Believers do not have the ability to produce spiritual fruit or eternal effect. At the same time, every believer can nurture the environment for growth in their own lives.

Imagine there are two deep ravines on either side of a narrow ledge. The ledge is the path of spiritual formation through the disciplines. To the right is moral bankruptcy through human striving. This is known as moralism. To the left is moral bankruptcy through liberty, called antinomianism (lawlessness). Only the ledge leads to God's transforming work from glory to glory and faith to faith.

### THE KEY OF BALANCE

Full awareness of our dependence on the Holy Spirit with full understanding of our responsibility to respond to His will is the balance that must be maintained. Overemphasis on either truth will disturb that balance.

Being totally dependence-conscious may create passivity, while total awareness of one's responsibility generates guilt and stress. Between those two poles lies the fruitful Christian life.

Note the passages of Scripture supporting each of these themes:

Dependence: "So then it is not of him that willeth, nor of him that runneth, but of God that sheweth mercy" (Romans 9:16; Ecclesiastes 9:10-12; 2 Corinthians 3:5, 6; John 3:27; 6:63; 15:5; Jeremiah 10:23; 2 Corinthians 12:9, 10; Proverbs 3:5, 6; Zechariah 4:6).

Our Responsibility: "Having therefore these promises, dearly beloved, let us cleanse ourselves from all filthiness of the flesh and spirit, perfecting holiness in the fear of God" (2 Corinthians 7:1; 2 Timothy 2:21; 1 Thessalonians 4:4; 1 Peter 3:15; 2 Peter 1:5-8; 1 John. 1:7; Colossians 3:5; Philippians 2:12).

Grace: "For it is God which worketh in you both to will and to do of his good pleasure" (Philippians 2:13; Colossians 1:29; 1 Corinthians 15:8, 9; Hebrews 13:21; 1 Corinthians 15:8-10).

### ORIGEN'S METAPHOR OF GRACE AND WORK

Our life is like a ship on a voyage. The wind is like God's

hand moving us in His will. We, as the captain, must work with the wind to set the sails for movement. Without the wind our work is fruitless; without our cooperation the wind's power is wasted in directing our lives.

## LOVE

Spiritual disciplines are not works to obtain righteousness, but a love relationship where the suitor takes advantage of every opportunity to be in the presence of the object of his love. Henry Nouwen said it well:

> This eternal community of love is the center and source of Jesus' spiritual life, a life of uninterrupted attentiveness to the Father in the Spirit of love. It is from this life that Jesus' ministry grows. His eating and fasting, his praying and acting, his traveling and resting, his preaching and teaching, his exorcising and healing, were all done in this spirit of love. We will never understand the meaning of Jesus' richly varied ministry unless we see how the many things are rooted in the one thing: listening to the Father in the intimacy of perfect love. When we see this we will also realize that the goal of Jesus' ministry is nothing less than to bring us into this most intimate community.[13]

### MARY AND MARTHA

The contrast between the two sisters of Lazarus clearly describes the contrasting motivations of love or law. Martha was full of duty, faithfully serving in the kitchen, carrying out the tasks she felt were urgent. Mary though, close to Jesus, was content listening, worshiping, and adoring in the Master's presence. She, too, felt the press of the urgent, yet she chose the important first.

Jesus said, "Martha, Martha, thou art careful and troubled about many things: But one thing is needful: and Mary hath chosen that good part, which shall not be taken away from her" (Luke 10:41, 42).

## CALL TO HOLINESS

**Objective:** The individual will demonstrate an understanding of the processes of spiritual formation with regard to the biblical *call to holiness* by discussing two views of this call.

"Be ye therefore perfect, even as your Father which is in heaven is perfect" (Matthew 5:48).

"But as he which hath called you is holy, so be ye holy in all manner of conversation; Because it is written, Be ye holy; for I am holy" (1 Peter 1:15; Leviticus 11:44).

## THE CALL TO SEPARATION FROM SIN

This call is most familiar since it has been the emphasis of Christian history in the last two centuries.

This biblical theme is identified by passages such as 2 Corinthians 6:14-17, "Wherefore come out from among them, and be ye separate, saith the Lord." The word "holy" from the Greek *hagios*, means "sacred (physically pure, morally blameless or religious), consecrated."[14]

Certainly there is the element of absence of sin or defilement in this definition. But more prominently, the idea of separation from sin came from the Old Testament background of the temple, sacrifices, and the tabernacle. There priests must not touch things unclean, sacrifices must be clean without defilement; and no unclean thing could come into the holy areas.

Mistakenly, the idea arose that righteousness could be defiled by proximity to sin. In "Be not overcome of evil, but overcome evil with good" (Romans 12:21), the thought is present that evil might overcome good. The implication from an Old Testament mindset would be not to allow evil to touch or defile oneself. In New Testament days this was seen in the Qumran community, which separated itself from society to be the pure and holy people of God.

The life of Jesus clarifies this extreme view of holiness as separation from sin. Though Jesus was without sin, He is regularly seen through His life with sinners. As a matter of fact, this disturbed the religious leaders of His day. They would not allow their reputations to be sullied by eating or socializing with sinners, yet Jesus did.

He demonstrated that holiness is separation from sin within the heart, rather than external rituals or observances of cleanliness and purity.

## THE CALL TO CONSECRATION TO GOD

From a more positive approach, holiness is the call to complete consecration to God. This is also seen in the Old Testament structure of Israel's worship. The Levitical priesthood was to be totally given to the Lord and the work of the temple. They did not own land or work to provide for themselves. Their full devotion was to be given to the labor of the worship of God (Leviticus 21:6: Numbers 8:16).

The Nazarites mentioned in the Old Testament were another illustration of this type of consecration (Numbers 6:2). This family committed themselves to a vow unto the Lord never to drink wine or any strong drink, and never to participate with unclean things. They were fully consecrated to the Lord. In a similar way the entire nation of Israel was like this as well. In God's eyes they were His chosen people. "For thou hast confirmed to thyself thy people Israel to be a people unto thee for ever: and thou, LORD, art become their God" (2 Samuel 7:24).

God redeemed them with the purpose that they would be the nation in all the earth that belonged to Him.

Now in the New Testament the call of holiness speaks this truth of consecration to all believers. Perhaps 1 Peter 2:9 says it most profoundly: "But ye are a chosen generation, a royal priesthood, an holy nation, a peculiar people; that ye should show forth the praises of him who hath called you out of darkness into his marvellous light." Believers are to be fully devoted and loyal to God in holiness. We are to be holy vessels for His use and glory alone. We are His people whom He desires to be completely given only to His will. One scholar wrote that the word "peculiar," used above, could be described as a circle which has only one dot right in the center. God's people are the dot in the center of His attention, redeemed to be His alone.

## HINDERANCES TO PERSONAL PIETY

1. A selfish attitude toward sin; egocentricism. Sin is an offensive act against God; it violates His will; it grieves Him. The goal must become weeping over sin and glorifying God through obedience to His commands.

2. Differentiating between sins. Most believers have their particular sin categories. Most overlook or ignore the list of more inward sins, such as Ephesians 4:31. And most forget to judge themselves before condemning others. In comparison to the majesty and holiness of God, all fault and failing is sin and needs His atoning power. In His heart all sin is grievous, not just our pet few.

3. Misunderstanding faith. Often believers think faith is believing with no action on their own. Popular concepts of faith focus on intellectual assent. Accompanying this is a feeling that all effort is of the flesh and cannot benefit the spirit.

Listen to Luther's words on faith: "[Faith] is a living, well-founded confidence in the grace of God . . . [It] makes its possessor joyful, bold, and full of warm affection toward God . . . Such a man becomes without constraint willing to do good to all."[15]

What a strange kind of salvation do they desire that care not for holiness . . .They would be saved by Christ and yet be out of Christ in a fleshly state . . .They would have their sins forgiven, not that they may walk with God in love, but that they may practice their enmity against Him without any fear of Punishment."[16]

## HISTORY OF SEEKERS

**Objective:** The individual will demonstrate an understanding of the processes of spiritual formation through *history* by discussing movements known for piety.

### Early Ages
*Monasticism*—(fourth century). The forerunners of this movement were the Desert Fathers who fled the then royal church of the empire to find God in the isolation of the desert. Often these men would return to civilization where they ministered, at times with supernatural interventions. Later the movement was organized in many societies such as Benedictines and Franciscans. They were known for their vows of poverty, chastity, and obedience. Often these cloisters brought spiritual renewal. Of course, the monastic movement was plagued by extremes, abuses, and failures through the centuries, yet it remained the main source of renewal through the twelfth century.

### Pre-Reformation
*Waldenses*—(thirteenth century). One of the first groups to apply the life of Christ beyond the priesthood to the common people. They sent people out two by two to preach and explain the Scriptures. They were early echoes of the back-to-the-Bible movement that would later shape the Reformation.

*Lollards*—(fourteenth century). These were followers of John Wycliff, who is known for printing Bibles with the intent of placing them in the hands of the common people. The Lollards went about preaching and teaching to the common people. These "poor priests" soon filled the land with their preaching.

*Hussites*—(fourteenth century). After Wycliff's impact came John Huss in Bohemia. Under the influence of Wycliff's movement Huss also incited people to return to the Bible and proclaimed Christ. After his martyrdom, the Hussites remained as a root in a dry ground till the Reformation, clinging to the Bible for all men and the evangelical proclamation of the Word of God.

## Post-Reformation

*Mennonites*—(sixteenth century). From the founders known as Anabaptists these reformers arose for New Testament spirituality, baptism, separation of church and state, and biblical living. They were what was called the radical wing of the Reformation who sought deeper changes than Luther or Calvin promoted.

*Puritans*—(seventeenth century). These reformers preached personal and national righteousness in England. William Tyndale had given his life to produce Bibles for the common man of England, and his fruit was the Puritan growth and influence. They believed they could meet as the New Testament believers in house groups to hear the Word and pray without the presence of a Church of England bishop. They were "preachers of personal and national righteousness."[17]

*Wesleyans*—(eighteenth century). This was a poor man's revival through England as the Church of England failed to minister to the needs of the abused working poor. They believed in a disciplined life aided by bands of believers who would meet to worship, study, and to hold one another accountable for personal piety. It was part of the Great Awakening move. Many historians feel that the Wesleyan revival rescued England from the same fate which France had suffered in the French Revolution.

*Pietists*—(eighteenth century). Soul hunger prodded this group to oppose the nationalistic and nominal faith of the German Lutherans. They believed faithful believers should gather in intimate fellowships. Laymen were encouraged to lead fellowships and proclaim the gospel. The Pietists emphasized care of souls, preaching and pastoral visitation, encouraged ministry of a revived spiritual laity, and enriched church music with their worship songs.

*Moravians*—(eighteenth century). These believers deeply influenced Wesley on his voyage back from America by their deep faith and calm in the midst of a storm. They are known as the first large-scale missionary-sending movement. Though small, the Moravians kept a continuous prayer going for over one hundred years. In proportion to their size, their mission zeal and activity still amaze believers and are a milestone in mission history.

It has been said of the reformers, "If justification was the apple of their eye, sanctification was their blind spot." In Adolph Harnack's oft-quoted statement, they "neglected far too much moral problem, the 'Be ye holy, for I am holy.'" In their reaction against the works religion of medieval Catholicism, the Reformers went too far and failed to do justice to the New Testament teaching of the Spirit and His work of sanctification. The result tended to be a strong emphasis upon orthodoxy to the neglect of a healthy doctrine of holiness and Christian spirituality.

Is this why widespread spiritual revival did not accompany the Reformation? The foundation was there, to be sure, but it was left to groups like the German Pietists, the Quakers, and the Moravians to attempt the superstructure of a Spirit-filled church. It was the church's great loss that Luther and Calvin were unable to overcome their Augustinian pessimism concerning the possibilities of grace. By failing to develop a full-orbed teaching of sanctification, the Reformers left a spiritual vacuum in Protestantism.[18]

**RECENT EVENTS**

*Higher Life and Holiness Movement*—Dissatisfied with denominational churches' inability to generate spiritual life and fervor, this movement used the camp meeting to stir the spiritual fires of both England and the USA. Again, there was a thrust back to the Bible and momentum to restore New Testament Christianity.

*Pentecostal Movement*—Out of the fires of holiness another flame burst forth, the outpouring of the baptism of the Holy Spirit. This movement brought yet another renewal to

Christianity emphasizing revival and personal experience of power through the Spirit. Ministry in the miraculous was revived in a prominent way in this time.

*Charismatic Movement*—A continuation in many ways of the earlier Pentecostal revival, the charismatic movement has spawned faith and supernatural ministry around the world. Church planting and mission activity have been unprecedented under its influence. World harvesting has been a significant theme under the leadership of the Holy Spirit.

## ABUNDANT LIFE

**Objective:** The individual will demonstrate an understanding of the processes of spiritual formation in the experience of *abundant life* by defining and discussing this life.

"The thief cometh not, but for to steal, and to kill, and to destroy: I am come that they might have life, and that they might have it more abundantly" (John 10:10).

"Jesus saith unto him, I am the way, the truth, and the life" (John 14:6).

"And you hath he quickened, who were dead in trespasses and sins" (Ephesians 2:1).

### EMPHASIS OF RESURRECTION IS LIFE

The offer of the New Testament Church was a new life, a qualitative difference in living. This fueled the attractiveness of their evangelism and the willingness of the messengers. They believed they had the answer to the world's needs, and they effectively demonstrated it.

The New Testament believers were known for their quality of life. Jesus was not widely known as He is today. Christianity was not a large and powerful mass of people numbering in the millions as it is today. Yet the simple, distinct life of those early believers mightily witnessed to a new opportunity to live in a world of oppression and fear.

Unquestionably one of the great appeals of the Early Church was the simplicity of life-style marked by the disciples. They were known for their love, even toward those who bitterly persecuted them. They were characterized by their infectious joy and praise. They displayed peace in the midst of untold pressures. They never ceased to show generosity towards the poor and afflicted. They exhibited a high moral standard which gave integrity to their message. They were loyal citizens, apart from refusing to call Caesar Lord. Of course there were blots and blemishes. But in general the simple and moral beauty of this new society, so utterly different to the pagan standards of the Roman world around them, earned them the title of the third race."[19]

The New Testament believers offered life in the present, not just a future hope of a different existence, an escape from the world's power in the afterlife. They demonstrated and boldly proclaimed that the life they were experiencing was the answer for the world's dilemma.

Today evangelism's focus is centered on the afterlife. Could this be because we have lost much of the reality of the new life available now? When there is little to demonstrate in the way of qualitative differences in living between the lost and the redeemed, evangelism must use alternative approaches to promote its claims. That has happened in this century. Assurance after life has replaced new life.

The basis of evangelism today cannot be new life since it is a verifiable fact that the difference between believers and non-believers is insignificant.[20] This mentality is even promoted publicly by phrases such as, "I'm not perfect, just forgiven." Though much in such phrases is true, the underlying message is that no difference should be expected between the Christian and the lost. In contrast, the early believers boldly offered life and challenged the world to inspect.

Discipleship is about living, not about knowing or believing as defined in today's terms. Today, knowing is mental acquisition and believing is mental assent. On the other hand, new life is experiential and impacts one's existence as well as one's spirit and mind. Discipleship is the growing experience of relating with Christ.

### WHAT IS THIS LIFE?

*Life is power to relate with God.* Think about it. A plant is able to relate with its environment — it is alive. The same is true for a cell, a kitten, or a person. On a higher plane then, spiritual life is the power to relate with God, Who is Life.

It is not just that we are dead to certain things. But we are alive to God, in a love relationship with God. Because of His life we are able to be in communion with Him, in this present moment in history.[21] As the Shorter Catechism says, "What is the chief end of man? To glorify God and to enjoy Him for ever."[22] He is life, and relating in Him imparts that life. The spiritual disciplines provide for us the avenues for consistently relating with Him for impartation of life.

*The fall is deformed life.* In sin we are separated from God, and, therefore, separated from this life. We continue to have life, but it is a deformed type, as one with cancer, or with paralysis, or with blindness. Those individuals have life, yet to some extent it is deformed. We may move about in a normal routine of biological and soulish life, but it is less than full in the sense of God's intentions for life. There is more.

Plato wrote a piece called "The Cave" in his book *The Republic.* In the cave were a people who had never seen the outside world. They were captives below. The sum total of their perception of reality was life in the cave. To them this was life in its fullness. Similar to the victims in Plato's Cave who never knew the true light of the sun, deformed life never knows the true life in full. The deception is that reality becomes what one knows. Satan, the father of deception, beguiles people to believe that his life in darkness is the ultimate in living. In the reality of eternity, it is deformed.

*The highest activity of life is relating and communing with God.* It is here that life is at its fullest. It is here life is refreshed. This is true because God is the source of all life. He is life. We say that we have eternal life, yet, the fact is, we have Him and He is life. We have no life of our own. Life is in Him. This is the reason why spiritual life, actually the fullness of life, can only be defined as the power to relate with Him. In the communion of relating, life is repeatedly imparted. He is the Vine; we are the branches. Therefore, the spiritual disciplines which exercise one's life in relating with God take on primary importance.

*We can choose life!* The Bible clearly teaches this though we trip up, thinking it is symbolic language, and/or we fail to realize that it takes exercise. Note these verses of Scripture:

"For those who live according to the flesh (deformed life) set their minds on the things of the flesh, but those who live according to the Spirit (God relating) set their minds on the things of the Spirit. To set the mind on the flesh is death, but to set the mind on the Spirit is life and peace. For this reason the mind that is set on the flesh is hostile to God; it does not submit to God's law — indeed it cannot, and those who are in the flesh cannot please God" (Romans 8:5-8, NRSV).

"Do not be deceived; God is not mocked, for you reap whatever you sow. If you sow to your own flesh, you will reap corruption from the flesh; but if you sow to the Spirit, you will reap eternal life from the Spirit" (Galatians 6:7, 8, NRSV).

## HOLINESS OF GOD

**Objective:** The individual will demonstrate an understanding of the processes of spiritual formation as impacted by *the holiness of God* by defining *qodesh,* Hebrew for "holy," and discussing implications for personal holiness.

"And one cried unto another, and said, holy, holy, holy, is the LORD of hosts: the whole earth is full of his glory" (Isaiah 6:3).

*William M. Greathouse,* From the Apostles to Wesley, *pp. 19-24*

Biblical theology has demonstrated conclusively that holiness is not merely one of God's attributes or even the chief moral attribute. Typical of the best biblical scholarship is the position of E. Jacob, who writes, "Holiness is not one divine quality among others, even the chiefest, for it expresses what is characteristic of God and corresponds precisely to His deity."[23] Supportive of this statement is an observation by Snaith: When the prophet says in Amos 4:2 that Jehovah "hath sworn by his holiness," he means that Jehovah has sworn by His Deity, by Himself as God, and the meaning is therefore exactly the same as Amos 6:8, where Amos says that "the Lord hath sworn by himself."[24]

A student of rabbinic literature observes that the most frequent name for God among the rabbis is "the Holy One." This reflects the prophetic name of God, "the Holy One of Israel."[25] Aulen states that: "Holiness is the foundation on which the whole conception of God rests. . . .In addition, it gives specific tone to each of the various elements in the idea of God and makes them a part of the fuller conception of *God*. Every statement about God, whether in reference to His love, power, righteousness. . .ceases to be affirmation about God when it is not projected against the background of His holiness."[26]

The Hebrew word for holiness is *qodesh*, which, with its cognates, appears more than 830 times in the Old Testament.[27] Scholars find three fundamental meanings in *qodesh*. (1) Often it carries the idea of "breaking forth with splendor." "There is no clear distinction between holiness and glory."[28] (2) The word also expresses a cut, a separation, an elevation. (3) *Qodesh* probably came from two roots, one which means "new," "fresh," "pure." Holiness means purity, whether ceremonial or moral. Cleanness and holiness are virtually synonymous ideas.

As God, He shines forth with glory peculiar to Himself. He was manifest in the burning bush, the pillar of fire, and on flaming Sinai. Of the tabernacle the Lord said, "It shall be sanctified by my glory" (Exodus 29:43). "I will be sanctified in them that come nigh me, and before all people I will be glorified" (Leviticus 10:3). In the lofty vision of Isaiah the account reads, "Holy, holy, holy, is the Lord of host; the whole earth is full of his glory" (Isaiah 6:3).

As God, He is separate from all creation. Holiness is the very nature of the divine, that which characterizes God as God and evokes worship from man. God is the "Wholly Other," standing apart from other, imaginary gods. "There is none holy as the Lord: for there is none beside thee" (1 Samuel 12:2). God's holiness means His differentness, His uniqueness as Creator, Lord, and Redeemer. Brunner says, "Only He who says, 'I, even I, am the Lord, and beside me there is no Savior' — can be 'the Holy One of Israel.' "[29] Yet His transcendence and separateness do not mean remoteness. As Snaith observes, "God was from the beginning transcendent in that He was different from man, but He was by no means transcendent in that He was remote from man. *I am God, and not man: the Holy One in the midst of thee* (Hosea 11:9). . . .Transcendence does not mean remoteness. It means otherness."[30]

As God, He is sublime purity. It is impossible for the Holy One to tolerate sin. In Genesis He is concerned with the evil imagination which pervaded mankind (Genesis 6:1-6). God's holiness is perturbed by the chronic perversity of man's heart (Jeremiah 3:17, 21; 17:9, 10). He is of purer eyes than to behold iniquity

(Habakkuk 1:13). When the prophet glimpsed God's holiness, he cried out, "Woe is me! for I am undone; because I am a man of unclean lips, and I dwell in the midst of a people of unclean lips" (Isaiah 6:5). Later Isaiah exclaims, "Who among us can dwell with the devouring fire? Who among us can dwell with the everlasting burnings?" (33:14, *RSV*). God's holiness is a devouring fire which will either purge away our sin or destroy us with it! As Jesus warned, "Every one shall be salted with fire" (Mark 9:49) — either the refining fire which makes us holy (Malachi 3:2, 3), or the wrath which destroys us (Malachi 4:1).

> "God is holy — as the Absolutely Pure, Resplendent, and Glorious One. Hence this is symbolized by the light. God dwelleth in light that is unapproachable. . . And Israel was to be a holy people as dwelling in the light, through its covenant-relationship to God. It was not the selection of Israel from all other nations that made them holy, but the relationship to God into which it brought the people."[31]

Walter Eichrodt says, "the decisive element in the concept of holiness is shown to be that of belonging to God."[32] George Turner adds, "Of God it is said, 'His way is perfect' (Psalm 18:30); but the God-fearing man also should, indeed must, 'walk with God' in this 'perfect way' (Psalm 18:32, 101:2, 6)."[33] "One way of expressing [holiness] in the Old Testament was the metaphorical expression of 'walking with God' in fidelity and fellowship. Enoch 'walked with God' (Genesis 6:9), in contrast to his neighbors. Abraham was also commanded, 'Walk before me and be thou perfect' (Genesis 17:1)."[34]

The New Testament continues this theme of relating and holiness with such passages "For this is the covenant that I will make with the house of Israel after those days, saith the Lord; I will put my laws into their mind, and write them in their hearts: and I will be to them a God, and they shall be to me a people" (Hebrews 8:10)."I will receive you, and will be a Father unto you, and ye shall be my sons and daughters, saith the Lord Almighty. Having therefore these promises, dearly beloved, let us cleanse ourselves from all filthiness of the flesh and spirit, perfecting holiness in the fear of God" (2 Corinthians 6:16 ; 7:1).

With the exception of the Decalogue, probably no other Old Testament passage influenced the Jewish people so much as the *Shema*, which has been called the creed of Israel: "Hear, O Israel: The Lord our God is one Lord: And thou shalt love the Lord thy God with all thine heart, and with all thy soul, and with all thy might" (Deuteronomy 6:4, 5). Love is said to be the motive of the Lord's choice of Israel, and love proven by obedience, the proper response (Deuteronomy 7:6-11).[35]

To make possible this perfection in love there must be an excision of inner perversity. However, there is provision for drastic surgery to bring this about: "The Lord thy God will circumcise thine heart, and the heart of thy seed, to love the Lord thy God with all thine heart, and with all thy soul, that thou mayest live" (Deuteronomy 30:6). This becomes the great New Testament doctrine of heart-circumsion by the Holy Spirit (Romans 2:29; Colossians 2:12). By the circumcision of the heart and the removal of inward sin, perfect love is made possible for the people of God! This is John Wesley's doctrine of Christian perfection."[36]

## CELEBRATION

**Objective:** The individual will demonstrate an understanding of the processes of spiritual formation through *celebration* and worship by listing Scripture passages validating that man's purpose is to glorify God.

Celebration is at the Heart of the way of Christ. He entered the world on a high note of jubilation: "I bring you good news of a great joy which shall come to all the people," (Luke 2:10 ) . . . Jesus began His public ministry by proclaiming the year of Jubilee, Luke 4:18, 19. Equally penetrating is the realization that as a result we are called into a perpetual Jubilee of the Spirit.[37]

### CREATED FOR PRAISE

It is clear from the Scripture that above all other mandates we were created to give glory and honor to God through our lives. John describes this high call when he says, "for thou hast created all things, and for thy pleasure they are and were created" (Revelation 4:11).

Peter writes with the inspiration of the Spirit saying, "But ye are a chosen generation, a royal priesthood, an holy nation, a peculiar people; that ye should show forth the praises of him who hath called you out of darkness into his marvelous light." (1 Peter 2:9). Chosen, royal, holy, and peculiar are adjectives describing very positive qualities in the eyes of God. Still, the more powerful phrase of this verse tells us why we are so blessed. The purpose is to publish or celebrate His excellencies or virtues. We are blessed so that attention will be turned to Him. Believers are called out of darkness to "showcase" the excellencies of the One who delivered them.

Even in the everyday mundane activities of life this call is in effect. Paul wrote to the Corinthians and admonished them saying, "Whether therefore ye eat, or drink, or whatsoever ye do, do all to the glory of God" (1 Corinthians 10:31). Then to the Philippian saints Paul wrote prophetically declaring that one day all mankind, redeemed or not, will bow the knee and give God glory (Philippians 2:11). The ultimate purpose of man will be fulfilled in praise to God, the only question is when. Today the abundant life is filled with praise. One day even the damned life, condemned to eternal punishment, will utter a final praise.

## LIFE OF CHRIST

Jesus' life is filled with praise events. In His birth Mary proclaims her wonderful confession, "My soul doth magnify the Lord, and my spirit hath rejoiced in God my Savior" (Luke 1:46, 47). The angels sang "Glory to God in the Highest." The shepherds came and worshiped and returned "glorifying and praising God for all the things that they had heard and seen" (2:20). The wise men brought gifts "and fell down, and worshipped Him" (Matthew 2:11). He never rejected praise from those who recognized Him as the Son of God. His presence and ministry evoked such outbursts of the heart.

## NEW TESTAMENT CHURCH

At the ascension "they worshipped Him and returned with great joy: and were continually in the temple, praising and blessing God" (Luke 24:52, 53). What a picture of the church there in its infancy. Their Saviour was gone; still they were described by the phrase "great joy." We are familiar with the abundant praise and rejoicing in the record of Acts: 2:11; 46, 47; 4:23-25; 5:41.

## ETERNAL PRACTICE

From two glimpses of the throne of God in Isaiah 6 and Revelation 4 we quickly realize that worship goes on constantly there and will be a central activity of eternity. Consider the seraphim which never cease night and day saying "holy" about the throne. Why does this not become a mundane task, a torturous eternity? Try saying holy repeatedly for one entire minute. Not only do these angels never cease, they never tire or get bored, because with each new utterance they have fresh insight into the eternal holiness of God. He sustains eternal praise.

## HEART IN HIS PRESENCE

A heart that recognizes the presence of the Lord can do little but worship in one form or another. One may bow down in reverential awe or leap with exhilarating joy, but all is simply a response to His presence.

*This response is rooted in Jewish celebration.* The Hebrews understood the celebration of joy in their God. They filled their calendar, not with stuffy religious ritual, but with feasts and festivals which marked the significant landmarks of faith. They had seventeen root words for joy in the Hebrew language. Though a suffering people, they understood joy.

*Joy in the Lord is strength.* Simply studying the physical side of emotions will disclose that depression makes one sick, and rejoicing keeps one healthy. "For the joy of the Lord is your strength" (Nehemiah 8:10).

*His joy remains full.* Our joy is fickle. It changes with our moods. His joy is unchanging at all times. We don't have to psyche it up. "These things have I spoken unto you, that my joy might remain in you, and that your joy might be full" (John 15:11).

*His joy bears fruit.* Too many believers have confused religion and joy. Religion becomes to them a burden to bear, an obligation to fulfill. They miss the point. To the Galatians, weighted by law, Paul said, "the fruit of the Spirit is . . . joy."

*His presence is the key.* "In thy presence is fullness of joy; at thy right hand there are pleasures for evermore" (Psalm 16:11). The secret of joy is to be with Him.

*Joy is a command.* The reason He can command joy is the same reason He can call us to His presence. He knows the two are the same. Joy is where He is. "Rejoice in the Lord alway, and again I say rejoice" (Philippians 4:4).

*Therefore celebrate!* Satan would like to make people think being a Christian is the worst thing that could happen to them. Just look at many Christians. Mahatma Gandhi, the great leader of India's march to independence once said, "I would be a Christian, if it weren't for Christians." Joy may be more important than we think (Romans 2:24).

## THE BODY

**Objective:** The individual will demonstrate an understanding of the processes of spiritual formation with regard to the *body* by describing the implications of control and release.

> "The body as well as the spirit now yearns to tread the way of redemption that leads to Calvary. It too wants to expose itself to the scorching sun of God's holiness."[38]

### CONTROL

In the discussion of spirituality and the body two points of view typically surface. Control is often thought of as the negative side, though it has its role to fill in spiritual maturity and holiness.

The natural functions of the body can easily be swayed to extremes and sinfulness. Actually many sins are ultimately manifested as behavior which the body carries out. Though these are seen as an act of the body, in reality much more is involved. We must affirm that the natural functions in themselves are God-given and not evil.

The ancient philosophers called the strong desires within man "the passions" and illustrated them by a chariot driven by two raging horses. One was black and the other white, and they were named Anger and Desire. It was felt that all of life was controlled by one or the other of these desires.

There is no doubt that life can be powerfully controlled by bodily impulses if unchecked. Consider eating for example. Some people tend to have less resistance in this area and find their thoughts, schedules, relationships, and other areas of life are definitely influenced by this function. Any of the functions or senses of the body can be the vehicle for abuse.

When unrestrained, such impulses have a blinding effect. People do not realize they are becoming slaves to their own cravings. The spiritual impact of this control is real. Domination by any craving becomes slavery of the body over the life, over the person. Michel Quoist said, "If your body makes all the decisions and gives all the orders, the physical can effectively destroy every other dimension of your personality."[39]

Paul taught the principle of control. He said, "I keep under my body and bring it into subjection" (1 Corinthians 9:24-27)

That phrase *"keep under,"* seems awkward today, but it means "to hit under the eye (buffet or disable an antagonist as a pugilist), that is, to tease or annoy (into compliance), subdue (one's passions): Keep under, weary."[40] Apparently Paul was serious in his efforts to keep his body from dominating and ultimately destroying his spiritual growth and maturity. (1 Corinthians 3:1-3; 6:19, 20; Hebrews 5:12, 13.)

**RELEASE**

Release is seen as the positive side of the body and spirituality. Some who don't understand have humorously said, "You can only be really spiritual after you are very old or dead." We know that this is a fallacy. Through many centuries in Christian history devoted believers have abused their bodies in a multitude of ways to try to suppress its evil influence. They, too, were in error.

The Bible affirms the role of the body as a positive part of spiritual development. The fact that Adam and Eve were created by God with bodies prior to the Fall demonstrates that they are good and have a place in the work of God. The Incarnation reaffirmed the worth of the body as Jesus Christ became "flesh" for redemption of the world.

The importance of this is multiplied when one realizes that Jesus, in His resurrected state, continues to live in immortal bodily form. He did not return to the spirit realm of existence, but maintained His bodily existence as a forerunner for us. Our hope of resurrection is not abandonment of the body, but rather completion and fulfillment of the body.

Paul teaches the principle of release of the body to its natural fullness when he says, "the body is for the Lord and the Lord for the body" (1 Corinthians 6:13). He also helps believers to see that the fulfillment of the body is not just for after death or rapture when he says, "Know ye not that ye are the temple of God and that the Spirit of God dwelleth in you?" (1 Corinthians 3:16). Now, in this life, believers can experience the release of the body from domineering cravings and into an instrument of the Holy Spirit. What a contrast: your body can be a bag of warring desires or it can be a fine-tuned, high-precision instrument in the hands of the Spirit. That is release — from confusion and destruction to life and power.

Believers, in this body, can live in union with God daily (John 15:7). Spirituality, abiding in the presence of God, becomes the ultimate activity of the body and all lesser are deformed bodily functions. To be handicapped is to have less than full capability. As vessels of the Spirit that dwells within us continuously, twenty-four hours a day, we can live at full God-intended bodily capability. Less than this qualifies for spiritual and bodily handicapped status.

Oh, yes, spirituality is not futile, self-torturing excesses of strange religious activities. It can be play or hard work. Spiritual joy and delight in the body can grow to supersede the mere bodily cravings that once dominated. And then, finally, the ultimate existence of the body will be resurrection, release from frail limits of this life.

> The disciplines for the spiritual life, rightly understood, are time-tested activities consciously undertaken by us as new men or women to allow our spirit ever increasing sway over our embodied selves. They help by assisting the ways of God's kingdom to take the place of the habits of sin embedded in our bodies.[41]

## TEMPTATION

**Objective:** The individual will demonstrate an understanding of the processes of spiritual formation in the area of *temptation* by summarizing the teaching of James 1:12-15.

> "Blessed is the man that endureth temptation: for when he is tried, he shall receive the crown of life, which the Lord hath promised to them that love him. Let no man say when he is tempted, I am tempted of God: for God cannot be tempted with evil, neither tempteth he any man" (James 1:12-15).

God understands and expects that we will be tempted. This is apparent from the text. Believers are tempted. Jesus was tempted of Satan. If He is our example we can expect to be approached by the enemy as well. God did not tempt Christ, neither does He tempt us. God does test His children (1 Peter 1:5-7; 4:12) and He chastens them (Hebrews 11:6-11). God may allow temptation or testing, as in the case of Job, though He will never allow destructive temptation that we cannot bear (1 Corinthians 10:12, 13; John 10:10; 1 Peter 5:8). The goal of both is cleansing, refining, and spiritual maturity.

This is the reason the text says, "Blessed is the man that endureth temptation." One who has come through a temptation, "endured," has been blessed in several ways: He is victorious with strengthened faith after an attack of the enemy; He is matured in the respect that he has felt the force of a temptation and has stood firm; He has pleased God and glorified Him through his faithfulness, and surely the blessings go on. An overcomer's bold confidence in the face of temptation is an "evident token of perdition" to the enemy (Philippians 1:28).

The Scriptures mention a specific blessing that the overcomer will receive. It is the "crown of life." The most frequently given interpretation of this is that the overcomer will receive this crown in heaven. I would like to share another interpretation which does not contradict the first and can be a great motivation for godly living in the present.

I believe the crown of life is an immediate grace that an overcomer receives as he endures against temptation. Notice the text says, "when he is tried." As Christians stand up against the enemy and resist his temptations, I believe the Word shows they immediately receive infusion of life. They have glorified God, chosen His way over the deceptions of evil, and instead of the letdown of discovering sin's empty void, God holds for them the pinnacle of experience — life! — The "crown of life."

As an overcomer continues to resist temptation, the infusions of life become similar to a ladder of spiritual growth: first, temptation; second, overcoming; third, life infusion, and the cycle continues. This is how overcoming temptation can become an effective means of spiritual growth rather than a depressing situation. Each victory provides the grace for greater growth. If a believer catches this realization, temptation can be viewed as opportunity. Jesus' own temptation experience confirms this. Luke said, "And Jesus returned in the power of the Spirit into Galilee: and there went out a fame of him through all the region round about" (Luke 4:14). There is a correlation between resisting temptation and vitality in spiritual life. "But every man is tempted, when he is drawn away of his own lust, and enticed" (James 1:14). Lust is simply strong desire. That alone is not sin. Many strong desires are either virtuous or even God-given; that is, passion for godliness or the love of a husband for his wife. Yet lust is the door of opportunity for the enemy. Know this — every temptation is attached to some desire that is already present. This is the reason it is vital to place all of our desires in the hands of God and keep them there. Surrendered to Him, they cannot be used by Satan to attack us.

The trouble comes when believers feel they can "handle" some desire. As one man said concerning temptation, "The best way to handle one is not to handle it at all." In our own ability we cannot be overcomers and handle our desires, no matter how moral or strong-willed we are. There will be one, our weakness, which will trip us every time. Out of God's hand, unsurrendered, though thought to be controlled — Satan is at liberty to attack that desire.

The red-flag warning signal for all Christians should not be that we are under attack in temptation. That is far too late. By then our desire has been engaged by the strong lure of Satan's deception, and we are being "drawn away." By then we are walking in the flesh trying to hold out as long as possible, which is impossible given time. There is a double-mindedness at this point (1:8). We want to please God and be faithful while at the same time we are fixed on the attraction of the desire for that temptation. This is true regardless of what the temptation may be — word, thought, or deed.

The red-flag warning should be for all believers when we consciously realize that there is a desire we want to hold rather than place into God's hand. At that point we move from the Spirit-empowered source for defeating the devil to the self-empowered (if that word could fit here) flesh. Literally, that means no power, defenseless, and Satan has us where he wants us. It is now only a matter of time. Sooner or later, we will speak the words, embrace the poisonous thoughts, or act out the deed.

The word, enticed, in the text says it all — "trapped." The drawing away moves the prey to the trap. Most people are so blinded by the desire, the lure, and the fleshly rationalizations at this point, they aren't caught by the trap; they jump in, having given in back down the road. They leap for the "pleasure of sin for a season," and find that it is over before it started, void, and meaningless. But everyone is tempted when he is drawn away by his own desires, not surrendered to God, and trapped. The rest is history.

May I repeat, our desires must be placed in God's hands and left there. The warning signal is not temptation, but the consciousness that we are trying to hold a desire on our own. Let's use fishing as an example of a desire. It sounds harmless enough. By the way, any desire, ANY desire can try to control one's life. Fishing can go from a once-a-month excursion for relaxation to daily, almost hourly daydreaming, and finally, too frequent trips that rob family-time, ministry-time, and worst of all, devotional-time. Unfortunately the latter will be the first to go. Note that.

On the other hand, fishing given to God becomes an activity in which He participates. Rest and relaxation is godly (for example, Sabbath). Experiencing His creation solicits praise and awesome wonder. Family members and ministry disciples can be participants. Meditation, prayer, reflection, and solitude can become a part of this desire given to God. The desire becomes a growth vehicle. Soon Satan would never want to see you there every day. Your life would be too full of glory. He may try to wreck the boat or foul up the engine to keep you away. See what I mean?

> Seek ye first the kingdom of God [in your desires] and all these things [fishing too] shall be added unto you" (Matthew 6:33).

Then when lust hath conceived, it bringeth forth sin: and sin, when it is finished, bringeth forth death (James 1:15). Earlier it seems, I implied that enticement was the end, sin's destruction. It is not. Even at that deadly point there is hope for a believer (1 Corinthians 10:12, 13). Look around for God's way of escape. He doesn't give up on anyone even after he has fallen into sin (Galatians 6:1, 2). He is the Deliverer out of temptation, in temptation, or after falling to temptation. The correct response is always looking to Him (Hebrews 12:1-3).

The word "conceived" is interesting to me. The most common use of this word in my culture is in the context of childbirth. When the sperm from the male reaches the ovum of the female, there is conception in the joining. In temptation sin occurs, not when the act is committed, the Sermon on the Mount makes that clear, but is when the passion of strong desire, lust, seizes, or joins with the will, our intention for action. That joining is sin regardless of whether there is an act or not.

Of the sixteen times "concieved" is used in the New Testament, the majority of uses are translated "take."

Literally, the lust takes over in the will and in the life. The person becomes lust-driven rather than will-driven or even Spirit-led. Our best defense is not the alarm of lust seizing our will. The best indicator is to learn to discern when our will has just taken back something from the Spirit's domain.

This is an important message to spread throughout Christianity because statistics reveal that a great majority of believers are nominal. In this context that means they are living, for the most part, holding their desires on their own. They are literally easy marks for Satan's attack. Like a fox in the chicken pen, he can pick whom he chooses, almost at will, among these nominal believers. Is it any wonder Christianity has posed so little threat to the kingdom of darkness? God is calling for an army of overcomers to spread the message and to pull down the walls of darkness.

Resolved, never to do anything which I would be afraid to do if it were the last hour of my life.[42]

## CONDEMNATION

**Objective:** The individual will demonstrate an understanding of the processes of spiritual formation in struggling with *condemnation* by listing pertinent Scripture passages that give strength.

Resolved never to give over, or in the least to slacken, my fight with my corruptions, however unsuccessful I may be.[43]

Any training—physical, mental, or spiritual—is characterized first by failure. So a necessity of discipline is perseverance.[44]

### THE ACCUSER

Satan is well known in his role as the "accuser of the brethren" (Revelation 12:10). If he cannot stop a person from ministering, then he will do all that he can to accuse and condemn him until he drops out on his own. Since his dominion has been destroyed through the cross, and he has no authority, he is resigned to using accusation and deception to influence people. Still, he is cunning and quite successful. He finds weaknesses or sensitive areas of temptation and drives at them. And if, per chance, a minister should sin grievously, his accusations persist long after God's mercy has covered the blot. He is out to destroy, and ministering saints are his prime targets to accuse.

## OUR MERCIFUL GOD

Lamentations 3:22 says, "It is of the Lord's mercies that we are not consumed, because his compassions fail not. They are new every morning: great is thy faithfulness." Even when we think we are living holy and feel comfortable in our righteousness, God's Word says even then it is His mercy sustaining us or we would have to be consumed. It is not our goodness, but His mercy that we must lean upon. If this is true as we stand confident, it is more sure when we falter.

Too often believers have viewed God as the omnipotent One waiting, full of wrath, to catch the first person to step over the line. Of course, that is an extreme view which Satan can use to condemn. Our view must balance the holiness of God with the mercy of God. Either extreme will keep us from living in His complete will. If one's view is unbalanced (in most often seeing God in His wrath), fear, self-doubt, and condemnation will defeat him. On the other hand, if one thinks God is without wrath toward sin in believers, arrogance, insensitivity, or overt sin will often defeat him (Psalm 86:15; 136:1-8).

## THE CERTAINTY

There is one thing certain: no one is above the snare of Satan and temptation. Perfection is certainly not a position of which to boast. Sin as failure, commission, omission, secret, presumptuous, offense, mental, motivational, or volitional is lurking at everyone's door. We are all similar to Peter, when Jesus declared of him, "Satan hath desired to have you" (Luke 22:31).

"Whatever lofty spiritual plane you imagine that you are on, remember, Adam was in paradise when he fell. Before your increased knowledge and religious experiences make you overly self-confident, recall that Solomon wrote three books of Scripture; he actually gazed upon the glory of God, yet he fell. Yes, even in your deepest worship of the Almighty do not forget, in long ages past, Lucifer himself was once in heaven, pouring out praise to God."[45]

## CONVICTION

Holy Spirit conviction is not the same thing as condemnation. Jesus came not to condemn — that is Satan's job description — but to save. Still, as we grow in holiness and maturity with Christ, failing to please God will convict us as much or more than previous gross sin in our lives. And in these areas we can hide from the Spirit with Adam and Eve in the garden or we can run to the Advocate (1 John 2:1, 2). If we choose to hide, regardless of the rationalizations, we are committing the sin of quenching or resisting the Holy Spirit.

## CONSOLATION

God has used many imperfect people who repented and ministered fruitfully. John Mark abandoned the mission. Barnabas and Paul split in contention. James and John were power-hungry. Elijah doubted after Carmel. Moses struck the rock and murdered. Abraham and Isaac lied. Isaiah confessed he had unclean lips. David committed adultery and murdered the husband. The twelve ran away. The ancient Church fell away into the Dark Ages. The Kingdom of God is divided.

## THE REPENTANCE SOLUTION

First John 1:9 and 2:1, 2 join other verses of Scripture to teach us that God is more interested in salvation, restoration, transformation, and continued fellowship than He is with wrath and destruction. Those factors will have their day, but in this age of grace God is open to the repentant seeker.

May we remember, though, that repentance is not over till there is fruit. If I repent of lack of love, my repentance ought to tarry till my love for that person springs forth. In this light it is not a one-time, carte-blanche, quick fix. It is a state of the heart for change, change personally (transformation), and change spiritually (relational) with God. Repentance is the forerunner of new spiritual growth. To lead us into new areas of maturing, God must first break the fallow ground through conviction and repentance.

## BELIEVERS, SIN, AND RESTORATION

John said, "My little children, these things write I unto you, that ye sin not." John was serious about sin and the fact that Christians should not sin. His next phrase, though, is, "And if any man sin, we have an advocate." John realized believers did at times sin. He did not say they were lost, separated from fellowship with God. He called them to run to the Advocate, find restoration, fight for the fellowship with God by quickly repenting.

# HUMILITY

**Objective:** The individual will demonstrate an understanding of the processes of spiritual formation through *humility* — by describing its abuses and characteristics.

> Satan fears virtue. He is terrified of humility; he hates it. He sees a humble Christian and it sends chills down his back, for humility is the surrender of the soul to God. The devil trembles before the meek, because in the very area where he once had access, there stands the Lord.[46]

## ABUSES OF HUMILITY:

Humility is not accepting an inferior position placed upon a person by others, as with women or racism. This is bigotry, not the pinnacle of godliness — humility.

Selflessness is often misunderstood to be a complete loss of your person. This is taught in universalism where all is moving toward union with the universe. All personality and self is completely lost in the impersonal whole. God made us all as He chose. We are His distinct creation with eternal destiny not to be lost.

Self-abasement is wrong. Though it may have a super-spiritual ring to it, giving oneself to others is wrong because we can only give ourselves to God truly. Giving ourselves to any other entity is idolatry. This is only godly when the object of our abasement is God.

Manipulative self-sacrifice, giving to get or be seen as humble, is hypocrisy. To appear humble so that others will regard you as exalted means that in the heart the individual was always self-exalted.

Humility is not feeling guilty; God came to deliver us from guilt. Too often innocent believers have thought that humility was thinking of oneself as less than good or valuable. One who has God as Father and Christ as a joint-heir has something to feel good about and can yet be humble.

Heroic self-image is not humility either, but superiority masked.

Humility is seeing all people as beloved in the eyes of God and as equally important as oneself.

## THE RELEASE OF HUMILITY

Humility gives up the need to be above reproach. Humility mobilizes, not paralyzes. It is not a code to follow; it recognizes that but by grace we all are doomed sinners; it treats all as equal in the sight of God and, therefore, man.

Humility is able to admit freely we are wrong, knowing God loves unconditionally, and that we are all tempted to sin. Those who have been exercised for the grace of humility have no problem with self-doubt or guilt—the abuses of humility. They know their worth is not in themselves, but they also know the worthiness of Christ is theirs.

Humility frees us from judging others — one of the most pervasive sins. It helps us identify with the sin and the sinner. As Moody said, "But for the grace of God, there go I"; or Paul, "But by the grace of God I am what I am" (1 Corinthians 15:10). Humility allows the believer to see even the sinner as beloved equally to God, just as the saint. This is in stark contrast to the Pharisee.

Humility is liberating. We don't have to keep producing for or protecting our reputation. There is no pressure to look good in the eyes of others (John 5:44; 12:43). Humility gives a person only one to please and follow — God.

Humility knows that force is not effective against violence. If the world is to be changed, the promise of the Prince of Peace is that it will be by the adoption of a whole new set of values that stand in opposition to those in the world.[47]

## THE GROWTH FROM HUMILITY

The bigger in God we grow, the smaller we will be. The Greatest said, "I am meek and lowly." Holiness is a product of grace which comes from humility. James said, "But he giveth more grace. Wherefore he saith, God resisteth the proud, but giveth grace to the humble" (4:6). Jesus condemned hypocrites, never sinners. If we are humbled at our failings, we get grace; if we are self-righteous, He condemns.

Humility is the essence of all virtues, the base of holiness. The first step is admitting we are not as holy as we appear. The Holy Spirit reveals our sin not to condemn, but to humble us so we can receive more grace. Holiness is not rules, but forsaking pride, refusing to rationalize the condition of our hearts (Luke 18:9).

Deeper humility is delighting in our weakness even in spiritual fullness. In our struggles it is natural to admit we are weak. Humility readily admits weakness even in strength (2 Corinthians 12:9, 10). Jesus was meek and lowly.

Meekness was His way of life. Anyone can judge (be superior), but who will save (serve humbly) (John 3:17)?

## INDICATORS
1. Humility sees through God's heart that all are equally important.
2. Humility is willing to be transparent, to be vulnerable for Christ's sake.
3. Humility knows how to delight in weakness.
4. Humility seeks to identify with Christ, to abound or be abased.

Indicators of meekness are seen when a person is approachable, sensitive, open to corporate life, and easily edified.

Humility is difficult . . .is countercultural. . .wreaks havoc with all individualistic values . . .is not a "live and let live" attitude . . .calls for a renunciation of all the deep attachments that the world holds dear. . .has to do with taking and accepting radical responsibility.[48]

## BROKENNESS

**Objective:** The individual will demonstrate an understanding of the processes of spiritual formation with regard to the state of surrender by defining *brokenness.*

*Watchman Nee, The Release of the Spirit, pp. 9-37, 57-64, 83-88*

### ILLUSTRATION IN NATURE
It is only when the beautiful flower petals are plucked and crushed that they can be transformed into fragrant perfume. The leaf of the herbal plant will produce no healing balm until it is broken. The gold nugget looks very similar to any other golden stone until it is melted in the refiner's fire and purified into gold bullion. The exquisite diamond must be chiseled out of the coal ore by the expert hand of the craftsman. Nature repeatedly teaches man that to obtain the best value or the maximum potential, crushing is required.

### ALABASTER BOX
In New Testament days an alabaster box was a prized treasure. It was made of stone and carried valuable spices, often

reserved for burial of the owner. It was beautiful and had a purpose, but the greater purpose was the breaking of the box for the ointment to flow out and the fragrance to fill the house.[49]

The woman at the feet of Jesus vividly portrays this lesson. She was broken as she carried an offering to the Master. Jesus contrasts her state to those who had invited Him. Listen as He speaks to us, the religious hosts. "Seest thou this woman? I entered into thine house, thou gavest me no water for my feet: but she hath washed my feet with tears, and wiped them with the hairs of her head. Thou gavest me no kiss: but this woman since the time I came in hath not ceased to kiss my feet. My head with oil thou didst not anoint: but this woman hath anointed my feet with ointment" (Luke 7:44-46).

The words of a song speak the message of brokenness clearly:

*Broken and spilled out, for love of You, Jesus,*
*My most precious treasure, lavished on Thee.*
*Broken and spilled out, and poured at Your feet,*
*In sweet abandon, let me be spilled out*
*and used up for Thee.*

*Broken And Spilled Out* ©1984 William J. Gaither, Inc. CCLI 2629

## TREASURES IN EARTHENWARE

"But we have this treasure in earthen vessels, that the excellency of the power may be of God, and not of us" (2 Corinthians 4:7). It is often hard for man to remember which is the treasure. Though we are unique created beings made in His image, we are not the treasure. Under that confusion man desperately seeks to protect the vessel. If he succeeds, the excellency of God is obscured. When he yields to the breaking, God is seen and His glory shines forth.

## KERNEL OF WHEAT

Christians have the tendency to interpret this passage as a prophecy of the death, burial, and resurrection (John 12:23-26). But the context in which Jesus spoke these words clearly directs the message of breaking to the disciples as well. "He that loveth his life shall lose it." If our Lord modeled this principle, and if He has called His disciples to the same, we can expect no less.

The eternal value that God has planned in our destinies will only be realized by surrender to the breaking. In breaking us God is working for our good. Matthew 21:44 speaks about falling on that stone, Christ Jesus. Falling on Jesus is our abandoned surrender to the crushing pressures. It is joining Christ in Gethsemene to say, "Not my will, but thine, be done." It is placing our lives in His hands.

Yet we can prolong the tests that break us by resisting, wasting God's time, choosing our own way. That verse continues by saying, "On whomsoever it shall fall, it will grind him to powder." The choice is serious, and it is ours. Falling on Jesus means we are under the weight of crushing. It is not easy. However the alternative is far worse — the judgment weight from resisting His best.

## THE IMPORTANCE OF BROKENNESS

The body is the vessel of the soul of man, and the soul of man houses the spirit of man. The soul is accustomed to having free rein in the heart of the lost. That is to say, his spirit is dead and he is driven by his mind, will, and emotion. Now when the spirit is quickened at the new birth, it becomes the home of the Spirit of God. God's Spirit comes to dwell, and He wants to lead. This is new for the soul of the man.

It is natural for the soul to rise and struggle with the Spirit for control. But through the process of breaking, the soul of man is taught to rest in His leadership. This is actually release for the man because control by the soul is slavery and bondage. Alone it is powerless to liberate. Under the Spirit's hand the soul is led to the highest purpose of living, glorifying God.

The spiritual disciplines of devotional life give the Spirit place regularly to teach the soul how to follow, how to think rightly, how to chose rightly, and how to experience right emotions. In the breaking process, the soul and body are becoming surrendered to the Spirit to such an extent that ultimately He will be seen transparently through the man's life.

As believers understand this, they will be able to begin discerning where they are in this process personally. Some may sense that they are drawing near to complete Spirit preeminence. Some may sense there are many times the soul exerts its strong force over the Spirit. And some may honestly realize that the Spirit has little place for control in their lives.

## SUBMISSION OF THE SOUL TO THE SPIRIT

Jacob became a great illustration of this. He was the favored son of his mother, could do no wrong at Laban's, grew wealthy, and yet his life was plagued with the fruit of his unbrokenness. He came close when wrestling with the angel, but his struggle continued; he lost his wife and his favored son. Finally, in Egypt, we see a transformed man as he answers Pharaoh, blesses his sons, and heads the family of Israel in prosperity.

## COMMUNION

**Objective:** The individual will demonstrate an understanding of the processes of spiritual formation through *communion* with God by listing biblical descriptions of fellowship with God.

God deals with us to develop spontaneity. Our character development is His primary purpose. He guides us toward His image though He will not override. Suppose a parent were to dictate to a child each minute detail of his activity for the day. The child would become stunted, dependent, underdeveloped in that regime. God seeks to produce autonomous character, the capability of making right decisions.[50] He does this through fellowship.

### VARIOUS DESCRIPTIONS

The privilege of communion with God has been described and illustrated in many ways through the Bible. Here are a few for your further study:

*Rent Veil* — symbolized the access which had always been reserved for the restricted priesthood. Now, by Christ's work in the atonement, there is entrance into the holy place of God personally. "Let us therefore come boldly unto the throne of grace, that we may obtain mercy, and find grace to help in time of need" (Hebrews 4:16).

*Tabernacle* — was the description of the dwelling place of God in the wilderness journey as He abode with His people. Speaking of Christ's life in the flesh, the Incarnation, John says, "And the Word was made flesh and *dwelt* among us." That word literally means to tabernacle,[51] paralleling the Old Testament tabernacle of God. The message was that now God is with us in tabernacle anew.

Today Christ tabernacles (dwells) with us moment by moment through His indwelling Spirit. He is just as real and as present in this age as He was for the children of Israel who could daily look to see the pillar of cloud by day or of fire by night representing His presence. John said, "Even the Spirit of truth . . .ye know him; for he dwelleth with you, and shall be in you" (14:17). "Behold, the tabernacle of God is with men, and he will dwell with them, and they shall be his people, and God himself shall be with them, and be their God" (Revelation 21:3).

*Union* — is used less but is seen clearly in John 17, "That they all may be one; as thou, Father, art in me, and I in thee, that they also may be one in us" (v. 21). Also Paul emphasized this description of our fellowship with God by using the phrase, "in Christ." For him the believer's position "in Christ" was a powerful principle of salvation. Still, it was not just a position, it was also a daily practical experience that the believer could enjoy. In this regard it is a wonderful description of communion for the saints. "To whom God would make known what is the riches of the glory of this mystery among the Gentiles; which is Christ in you, the hope of glory" (Colossians 1:27).

*Sabbath* — describes not only the day, but also the truth that Christ is our rest. Our soul's tendency to become weary can be restored in His rest, in Him.

*Secret Place* — is the phrase used in Psalm 91. Here He is described as the protection, covering His children, assuring them, and keeping them.

Immanuel and Jehovah Shammah — are names used for Christ and God, respectively, which describe their presence in fellowship. Immanuel is "Christ with us." Jehovah Shammah means "the God who is there" (Hebrews 13:5, 6).

*Dallas Willard*, In Search of Guidance, *pp. 16-29*

## PERSONAL INTELLIGENT INTERACTION WITH GOD[52]

*Adam and Eve* — had experienced this in their garden life, though they were separated from such communion through the Fall. Now this fellowship is offered through redemption, and the resurrected Christ as the key to new life.

*Christ's Ordination* — in Mark 3:13-15 is a restatement, or a renewal of this invitation. Christ is calling disciples to the highest call of being with Him knowing that all other activity will be a byproduct of that communion. We may interpret this call to say that God is more interested in our abiding relationship with Him than our great ministry for Him. Too often in this pragmatic age we feel just the reverse, and come to Him mostly for our ministry, not His fellowship.

*Love* — is a way of being with another. This is the touchstone of our communion with God. He seeks a people to be with Him in love; domination by command is not compatible with such a relationship. It is nearly impossible for the authoritarian order or the attitude of superiority to find real friendship and fellowship among others.

*Spontaneity* — is a quality of godly communion. He prefers to relate with us by guiding while not overriding. He is more interested in the process we go through to make a choice than the actual choice itself. For Him, choosing a holy course simply to impress peers is no better than choosing the unholy choice. His interest is in the interaction and struggle for relationship as the choice challenges our living. He would be a tender Shepherd rather than a vicious sheepdog corralling His flock.

*Engaging Our Faculties* — is an aim of fellowship. God created us to think profoundly, feel intensely, and will with determination. He aims to heighten those qualities through divine interaction. He intends they be used in their peak and for His glory. Faith in Christ does not numb the emotion, dull the senses, paralyze the brain, or freeze our volition. A life of fellowship with Christ would do just the reverse, challenging every capacity which God has placed in man, His beloved creation. He has made us to relate with Himself and that our capabilities can be stretched and grown to the maximum potentials. Actually, only fellowship in Him frees us for this.

*Shared Activity* — is a sign of maturity. This is observable in children. In the early stages of development children do not relate in shared activity. They may play in the same space together. They may interact as needed. They may even feel more comfortable in the presence of other children. However, it will only be later, in maturation, that children begin to share activities with real interaction. God is seeking children who will mature in sharing their lives with Him in communication, which will spawn communion, which, in turn, will spawn union.

## WALKING IN THE SPIRIT

**Objective:** The individual will demonstrate an understanding of the processes of spiritual formation through *walking in the Spirit* by citing and discussing Bible passages illustrating this.

This I say then, Walk in the Spirit, and ye shall not fulfil the lust of the flesh" (Galatians 5:16).

And you hath he quickened, who were dead in trespasses and sins" (Ephesians 2:1).

### WALKING IN ANOTHER REALM

The Bible distinctly teaches that there are two realms of reality, or it might be more accurate to say two realms which make up complete reality. For example:

- "For we wrestle not against flesh and blood, but against principalities, against powers, against the rulers of the darkness of this world, against spiritual wickedness in high places" (Ephesians 6:12). Obviously this is speaking of reality outside of flesh.
- "While we look not at the things which are seen, but at the things which are not seen: for the things which are seen are temporal; but the things which are not seen are eternal" (2 Corinthians 4:18). The Bible distinctly states here that there is reality in the unseen.
- "Likewise, I say unto you, there is joy in the presence of the angels of God over one sinner that repenteth" (Luke 15:10). The two concurrent realities mentioned side by side.

Of course, when one begins to look in the Scriptures, the search could go on and on because it is quickly seen that the Bible is a book about two realities. They are not simply mentioned a few times, the two realities are the context of the message of this Book. Notice various real people and their experiences with the unseen: Gehazi, Elisha's servant, is terrified because the enemy has surrounded the town with the intent to take Elisha. It is then that Elisha speaks confidently, "Fear not: for they that be with us are more than they that be with them. And Elisha prayed, and said, Lord, I pray thee, open his eyes, that he may see. And the Lord opened the eyes of the young man; and he saw: and, behold, the mountain was full of horses and chariots of fire round about Elisha" (2 Kings 6:16, 17).

The context of the book of Job in its entirety is between the two realms of reality. Satan has come before God in the realm of the Spirit, and the rest of the book is set in such a way that God and Satan are in the background of that reality observing the actions of Job in the realm of the flesh. In a different way, the entire book of Acts repeatedly reminds the reader that the realm of the Spirit is regularly interacting with the natural world through the Apostles. It may be interesting to study the Bible with this in view.

## CLOSED UNIVERSE

In this century it has been the dominant view of science that the physical world was the sum total of reality and life. Though Christianity would like to believe that it cannot be influenced by secular forces such as science, that is not so. Science in this century has replaced religion and the Bible as the authority for living in the Western world. Therefore, when science declared that there was only one realm of reality, that became predominant in society. Certainly people continued to speak of God and use such language, but for the most part the concept behind the language changed to mean something very different, which would fit the idea of a closed universe.

I said this thinking has influenced believers. Though most continue to hold that the Bible is true and authoritative, the application of life in two realms shifted. Walking in the Spirit is a prime example. This term today is a religious cliche which is empty of real meaning or definition. Ask believers today how one walks in the Spirit. The term is still used, but it lacks practical force to motivate believers' lives. It has been stripped of its context: the reality of the realm of the Spirit, present but unseen. This has been the increasing dilemma for believers through this century until recently.

## OPEN UNIVERSE

More recently science has realized that the universe is not closed, but open. This amazing turnabout has made, and will continue to make, drastic changes in the way people view themselves and life. Dallas Willard writes:

> The current state of the physical sciences, in opposition
> to the crudely mechanical view that was dominant for sev-

eral centuries past, is very congenial to the view of God's presence in His world. . ."Today there is a wide measure of agreement, which on the side of physics approaches almost to unanimity, that the stream of knowledge is heading toward a nonmechanical reality; the universe begins to look more like a great thought than like a great machine. Mind no longer appears as an accidental intruder into the realm of matter; we are beginning to suspect that we ought rather to hail it as the creator and governor of the realm of matter."[53]

Recent trends demonstrate the response of society to this. First, stripped of their Christian foundation, individuals' concepts of God were shaken. Then after realizing that there was an entity beyond the seen realm, they were ripe for every cultish and occult doctrine possible. That is the reason why it is so urgent for believers to recapture their firm footing in the doctrine of walking in the Spirit. This new turn has made society ripe, as well, for the true explanation of the reality of the Spirit. He is the definitive answer to reality and life beyond the seen. We have the message that people desperately need to hear.

**THE SPIRIT, OUR JOINING**
The Spirit was called by Jesus "another Comforter" (John 14:16). Jesus was the primary Comforter to them. He was the God-sent Messiah in answer to the Jewish longings of centuries. By calling the Spirit "another Comforter" He was literally placing the Spirit in His role as He ascended to the Father. Therefore, what we see in Jesus in His earthly ministry we should now expect from the Spirit. To begin practically to apply that is life-transforming. It is what the Bible means when it uses the simple phrase "walk in the Spirit" (Galatians 5:16).
Jesus joined the disciples to God and His Kingdom physically and really. It was through Him they saw the power of the Kingdom, as well as its truths, life, love, mission, and all. Now, through this Person, the Holy Spirit, who is present with us though in the unseen, we have the same opportunity as the disciples — to walk with Jesus — to walk in the Spirit. It is not a mystical spiritual truth which we cannot actually apply. It is simple faith in God's Word, and believing that the Person, the Holy Spirit, is right now, right here, with us.

By faith we begin to live, aware that He is here. What should we do? Like the disciples then, let Him tell us by being sensitive to His promptings. What shall we say, and any other question, becomes a motive for further dialogue with Him and growth in sensitivity. This kind of life will take exercise and growth.

At times, like the New Testament writers realized in their converts, we will be out of the Spirit and then in the Spirit again. What does that mean? It relates to awareness, sensitivity, and yieldedness. At times we will not be aware of sensing Him or of being truly yielded. But as we grow in our walk in the Spirit, we will find we are more often aware of walking with Him. He is leading and becoming free to do His ministries through our lives. This is so much better than when we try to do His ministry by ourselves. It is His way.

## SPIRIT-WALK TRAINING

Some Bible scholars believe that Jesus needed to work with the disciples on this concept of walking in the Spirit as well. One explanation for the forty days after the resurrection when Jesus appeared several times is based on this. Could it be that Jesus knew that these men were not familiar with such an experience? Could it be that this concept was so important that Jesus realized they needed a transition time for training? For whatever reason, we know that the defeated group of men who hid nervously after the crucifixion stood publicly and boldly on the day of Pentecost to launch the evangelistic thrust for all history. They learned the lesson. He was with them in the Spirit.

## LOVE

**Objective:** The individual will demonstrate an understanding of the processes of spiritual formation with regard to *love* by listing Scripture references on this priority.

### THE GOAL OF LIFE

The goal of life for the early believer was love, and humility was the way to attain it. It was their powerful way of disarming a violent society. They had no political influence, no economic power, no massive social structure, but they had genuine love for God, for one another, and for the world. They touched their world without confrontation or revolution, but with love.

## LOVE IS PERFECTION

Wesley's definition of perfection is as yet unimproved and still carries the essence of what is meant by the term in holiness circles . . . At the end of the *Plain Account,* Wesley sums up his teaching in these words: By perfection I mean the humble, gentle, patient love of God, and our neighbor, ruling our tempers, words, and actions. He was careful to guard against a Pharisaic or legalistic view of perfection. . .For Wesley, as for scripture, Christian perfection means *perfect love.* This is the sense in which it has been understood by the clearest exponents of the teaching through the centuries. . . In his sermon on Christian perfection, Wesley therefore says, "It [perfect love] is only another term for holiness. They are two names for the same thing."[54]

## PERFECTION NEGATIVELY

The way we see perfection as a negative would have frightened the ancient Church fathers. The gospel is clear in its call (Matthew 5:48; 1 Peter 1:15, 16). They had no intention of a cold adherence to rules, nor utter freedom from temptation. Those tempted less were regarded as those God knew could stand little.

"But I say unto you, Love your enemies, bless them that curse you, do good to them that hate you, and pray for them which despitefully use you, and persecute you; That ye may be the children of your Father which is in heaven: for he maketh his sun to rise on the evil and on the good, and sendeth rain on the just and on the unjust. For if ye love them which love you, what reward have ye? do not even the publicans the same? And if ye salute your brethren only, what do ye more than others? do not even the publicans so? Be ye therefore perfect, even as your Father which is in heaven is perfect" (Matthew 5:44-48).

The perfection that will be patterned after the Father is perfection of love. That is the context of this passage. When verse 48 says, "Be ye therefore," the reference is to the preceding four verses where Jesus has described an amazing quality of love — a love which will love those that hate us. It is in love, an amazing love such as this, that Jesus calls us to the perfection of the Father. Perfection Was and Is Loving God With All the Heart.

The great commandment shows us the centrality of love. "Master, which is the great commandment in the law? Jesus said unto him, Thou shalt love the Lord thy God with all thy heart, and with all thy soul, and with all thy mind. This is the first and great commandment. And the second is like unto it, Thou shalt love thy neighbour as thyself. On these two commandments hang all the law and the prophets" (Matthew 22:36-40).

"And above all these things put on charity, which is the bond of perfectness" (Colossians 3:14). Paul says love is so vital that it is primary, it is the uniting principle in perfectness. If one hopes to be perfect, love is the glue that holds it all together.

"Now the end of the commandment is charity out of a pure heart, and of a good conscience, and of faith unfeigned: From which some having swerved have turned aside unto vain jangling; Desiring to be teachers of the law; understanding neither what they say, nor whereof they affirm" (1 Timothy 1:5-7). Note that the small word "end" is quite significant. It is the root from which the word "perfect" comes. We could say, "now the perfection of the commandment is. . . ." The target, the goal, the final destination where the commandment wants to carry us all is love.

"And above all things have fervent charity among yourselves: for charity shall cover the multitude of sins" (1 Peter 4:8). For the second time we see love connected with the phrase "above all things." If that really means what it is saying, you could place any other religious qualification beside love and love would take precedence every time. Think about that. Then it teaches us that love will cover a multitude of sins. Try to find anything outside of Christ in the Bible that will deal with sin, anything. Yet Peter says love has a profound effect even with sin.

Notice the priority of love all through the New Testament. First John 4:7-19 teaches quite a bit about this love. For instance, it says that if we love, we are born of God, and if we don't, we don't know Him. Apparently John thought that love was the supreme indication of whether a person was a Christian or not. Later he tells us that the person that dwells in love is really dwelling in God. And he caps it off by revealing that God is love. Is it any wonder that love means holiness, perfection, and maturity?

We must not forget that John 13:34, 35 teaches us that the most effective world-winning evangelism/mission strategy is love. Romans 13:8 says we ought to have only one debt to any man, to love him. Galatians 5:14 simplifies things greatly when Paul teaches us that all the law is fulfilled in one word, love.

Roberta Bondi, To Love As God Loves

*This love perfection did not seem repulsive.* It was God's call (Matthew 5:48; Luke 10:27). . . The ancient Church understood that fear was the hindrance of love, which blocked perfection as 1 John 4:17, 18 speaks of. Love casts out fear. . . Perfection is not a compulsive person, nitpicking, judging others, or a refusal to accept our sinfulness as fallen. Love expressed in humility was a way of seeing others as equally important as ourselves (Philippians 2:1-7). Humility was the path to love, and love, the key to all virtue.

*Love defeats legalism's self-righteousness.* Love identifies in compassion and works to heal rather than judging for criticism. Love is not duty or guilt, but a delight in God's love and responding by loving others.

*We gain greater freedom over appetites and emotions as we grow in love for God.* We are most human when we are fulfilling the design God had for us at creation, loving Him. So "I'm only human" is an error; we should say, "I'm fallen, but God can restore my humanity."

*We grow closer to God as we love others.* If God is the center of the circle and each radius is a person, we move toward God as we all go closer to one another. This is an extension of the great commandment which says to love your neighbor as yourself.

*Motivation reveals much.* First, people come to God out of fear, then they seek God for reward, finally, they come to God for the relationship of love in His communion. This is the highest, most mature, perfect worship.

*Love as emotion is short term at best.* Love as disposition or commitment usually takes over in marriage and becomes a way of life. It takes choosing love over other options repeatedly, and it takes practicing continually.

*Temperament and disposition are two ways of seeing this love.* Temperament is immature and will control, but in maturity the chosen and cultivated attitude of the heart will take control. Love, then, is the goal we are practicing to practice more.

*Covet command becomes the opposite of this perfection.* In many ways the last command is the ultimate. It is the most internal. It directly relates to our love for God. If we are loving (coveting) with our affection, it also means our affections are not totally given to God. Covet becomes the indicator in the negative of our affections.

## EVANGELISM

**Objective:** The individual will demonstrate an understanding of the processes of spiritual formation through *evangelism* by describing Jesus' outreach strategy.

Evangelism, it seems, took two forms in the New Testament and in the Early Church just as it did in the ministry of Christ: community and proclamation. At any point, when two categories are mentioned, the temptation arises for the two to be dichotomized. Some will focus on one while others will focus on the other, and through specialization of task misunderstandings may arise. In this important case the two must never be separated. They work hand in hand as Michael Green suggests:

> Unless there is a transformation of contemporary church life so that once again the task of evangelism is . . . backed up by a quality of living which outshines the best that unbelief can muster, we are unlikely to make much headway through techniques of evangelism. Men will not believe that Christians have good news to share until. . .they see in church grouping and individual Christians the caring, the joy, the fellowship, the self-sacrifice and the openness which marked the early church at its best.[55]

Jesus drew twelve men together to be with Him for His earthly ministry. This was the beginning of community. It would be the outworking of relationships in that group where seeds were planted for the Christian community, the Church, which was to be formed. Community has been lost to the Church in the flood of Western individualism and needs to be undergirded again if a vital witness is to flow out from believers in this age.

Proclamation, on the other hand, has gained popularity since the "Great Awakening" with preachers such as Spurgeon, Whitefield, Wesley, and Finney who made great advances for the kingdom of God preaching to the masses. The holiness camp meetings, pentecostal revivals, and the charismatic renewal all have made use of mass proclamation methods with great benefit. Along with these methods, personal approaches for proclamation have been birthed in the last fifty years and have motivated thousands to share their faith personally, winning the lost.

Proclamation works well in an environment where people have been prepared for the hearing of the gospel.[56] Therefore, in the post-reformation decades the "Great Awakening" proclamation thrived. In America, with its Christian heritage, the holiness movement, pentecostal movement, and charismatic movement have all flourished in a gospel-prepared society — people who are familiar with the tenets of the gospel and have been influenced by them to some degree.

Presently, evangelism in America is facing a growing dilemma. More and more of our nation has drifted from the Christian heritage of our past and has moved toward a post-Christian view of society. In that context it will be increasingly difficult for proclamation evangelism to operate. Evangelism will be forced to learn what missionaries have been learning through the decades when faced with a society where Christ is unknown or seemingly irrelevant to their context. The gospel is then carried on the strength of the Christian witness in the relationship the evangelist is able to initiate and maintain with the prospects. Relational evangelism becomes the priority, and community becomes a vital part of that witness. The community relationship between the evangelist and the prospect, the community relating of the small group of believers working to win others in that society, and the community relating between the believers and the larger world where they live, all become crucial to the success of the gospel. Once again the pendulum is swinging back toward a more balanced view of evangelism which embraces both proclamation and community for the spread of the gospel.

An illustration of the vitality and potential for outreach and growth when these two elements are combined can be drawn from Methodist history. "Clearly American Methodism was conceived as a missionary movement, calculated to win the greatest number of people in the shortest amount of time. And, as no other fellowship in Western Christianity, they did just that. Within one generation this fledgling sect, after its formal organization in 1784, grew from a few thousand adherents to the largest denomination in the land. It surpassed in size its nearest rivals, the Baptists, by twenty percent; and numbered as many members as all Episcopalians, Congregationalists, and Presbyterians combined. . . [Why?]. . .For the first hundred years of Methodism it would be hard to find in Christendom a more effective system of discipleship. . .[with] the organization of local societies into bands, classes and meetings of various kinds, cared for by their own lay leaders. Within the fellowship of these close-knit communities of faith, they ministered one to another in love. Each member found an unprecedented opportunity for spiritual and social development."[57]

Here is testimony to the potential when proclamation and community are balanced.

## DISCIPLESHIP

With this return to the importance of community and the recognition that it is foundational for proclamation, the ministry of Jesus again becomes the central model. What was the primary ministry strategy of Christ? What approach was uppermost in His ministry work? It has been shown that Jesus ministered to all types of people regardless of their status in society. He touched people personally in one-on-one encounters. He ministered when there were groups, crowds, and multitudes of people coming to see and hear His ministry. Jesus ministered in a variety of settings and ministry styles. He reached people and touched people wherever He was.

"The program of Christ's own ministry determines the program He has appointed for the ministry of the church."[58] The Synoptic Gospels paint the picture of Jesus involved in all the ministries mentioned while at the same time carrying out His primary ministry objective. Howard Belben, in *The Mission Of Jesus*, says, "Jesus was able to command the attention of multitudes who at times travelled great distances to hear Him and watch Him heal the sick. But though He gave them the attention and care, the teaching and healing they wanted, the top priority for Him clearly seems to have been the training of the few."[59]

It was, in fact, a part of His primary ministry, "the training of the few," which led Him to go to the people in all their various settings. He was modeling ministry and equipping the twelve while He was ministering to the public. With this understanding it can be said that all of Jesus' ministry focused on developing the men He had chosen. Ministry to His chosen community (the twelve) motivated all His other ministering.

Was this ministry strategy continued by the men Jesus had trained? Did they understand Jesus' purposes and utilize them in their own ministries as His apostles? Did they understand the Great Commission in terms of the Lord's model and call to "Go ye into all the world and *make disciples* of every nation" (Matthew 28:19)? It is not possible in the scope of this work to study the life and ministry of each apostle. Yet Paul gives us opportunity to look at his strategy for ministry and compare it with that of Jesus. In 2 Timothy 2:1, 2, Paul counsels his "son in the faith," and urges him to minister as he has done. He said, "Thou therefore, my son, be strong in the grace that is in Christ Jesus. And the things that thou hast heard of me among many witnesses, the same commit thou to faithful men, who shall be able to teach others also."

Here is Paul, thought of as the greatest missionary of Christian history, the man inspired to write more of the canon than any other. He is writing his last letter to Timothy. He is in prison and seems reconciled to the fact that his life is near the end. It is in this letter that he says, "I have fought a good fight, I have finished my course, I have kept the faith: Henceforth there is laid up for me a crown of righteousness, which the Lord, the righteous judge, shall give me at that day" (2 Timothy. 4:7, 8). In this same letter Paul gives Timothy his strategy for ministry.

## COMMITTING: LIFE POURING

The most important word Paul uses to convey his ministry strategy to Timothy is the word "commit" (2 Timothy 2:2). The meaning is literally "to pour into." This idea can be described by the image of pouring water from one vessel into another. Paul has poured into Timothy, his dear son in the faith, the things that have been given to him from God. His letter mentions this in the phrase, "the things that thou hast heard of me among many witnesses." From the life and heart of Paul to the life and heart of Timothy, spiritual revelations, insights, and learning has passed.

Now Paul is challenging Timothy to select "faithful men" into whom he will be able to pour these riches. Timothy will now do as Paul had done with him, he will pour from his life the revelations and inspirations he had personally received into the lives of others. Paul also gives the indication that this process is not to stop with Timothy's men. He encourages Timothy to find faithful men so that they "will be able to teach others also." The strategy is intended to continue. It is possible that from his prison captivity Paul was able to see third- and fourth-generation leaders being discipled through those into whom he had "poured."[60] In this instruction we sense Paul calling the Church to be disciplemaking communities, constantly pouring life from God.

Here we see the ministry of Jesus repeated in the discipling relationship of Paul to Timothy. It was this same program Jesus pursued as He spent three years with the twelve men He had called out to "be with Him." From the life of Jesus poured calling, vision, and modeling to the twelve chosen to carry on His work when He had ascended. All that He did in those crucial three years was intended for the disciples' learning and ever-growing awareness of His eternal work. He could have established a kingdom. He could have gathered a people to Himself. He could have organized a religion full of followers. He was certainly popular enough with masses thronging to Him in increasing devotion. Yet the twelve were the goal of His work. They were the object of His pouring, His discipling community.

Jesus would not dilute His powerful ministry strategy by accepting the less-consecrated, less-serious masses. The account in Luke 14 demonstrates this well when Jesus three times tells the crowd around Him, "You cannot be my disciples" (Luke 14:25-33). Preceding each of these declarations Jesus has given them a hard saying to consider: except they forsake all, except they hate father and mother, except they take up their cross. He was not interested in gathering multitudes who would clamor for Him. His ministry goal was to pour His life into twelve men. That small, but consecrated community of disciples was His primary focus. He knew that the world would be touched through such a strategy. It was the only way.

From the observation point of history, almost two thousand years removed, we can see that His strategy did work. "By A.D.

300 the church had shown such tremendous strength and virility, and was spreading so swiftly, that it appeared the entire civilized world could be evangelized by A.D. 500."[61] The Bible concurs from the witness of certain envious Jews who did not believe the gospel (Acts 17:5, 6). Their cry was that they "that have turned the world upside down are come hither also." So it was that Christianity began as a tiny offshoot of Judaism and became, in three short centuries, the favored, and eventually the official, religion of the Roman Empire.[62]

## EQUIPPING

**Objective:** The individual will demonstrate an understanding of the processes of spiritual formation through *equipping* by defining equipping the saints.

What happened? If in the last section the Christian faith was on the brink of conquering the world at A.D. 300, what brought this vibrant movement to a standstill? What caused the accelerating growth of the Church to diminish?

Many believe the most damaging blow was the downfall of the ministry of disciplemaking by each believer. The zealous spread of the life of Christ from one life to another through disciplemaking had been the key to growth and continuity. With the Edict of Toleration, Constantine's embrace of the Christian religion, and many other edicts and events favoring the Church, Christianity moved from the catacombs into the Roman palaces and grand basilicas.[63] Popularity was one temptation Jesus discerned as destructive. The third century Church was not so discerning. The influx of pagan Roman citizens into the new religion of the empire flooded the Church. Gone was the sincere pure worship in the community of the faithful who risked their lives to fellowship with one another. Gone was the simple discipling call for each believer to pass on this life to another and to minister till maturity was realized.

Now the worshiping masses in beautiful basilicas knew little of the gospel and relied totally on the clergy offices to lead them in performing the religious acts associated with faith. With such additional responsibility over the worshiping throngs, the clergy offices were elevated. Soon the work of religion was seen as the responsibility of those clergy offices, and the common believer was expected to do little, lacking knowledge. With this separation of the clergy and laity, the New Testament example had been compromised. The priesthood of believers had been neutralized. The witness of the laity had been immobilized. The ministry strategy of Jesus had been overwhelmed. This movement that Satan could not stop through severe persecution he disabled with a flood of popularity and acceptance. The tightly-knit communities of believers who had received personal equipping from mature and dedicated saints were vanishing.

Today the clergy-laity split is still evident. A passive mentality pervades congregations while the ministry is expected to be active and responsible in the functions of religion. The laity sits as a sleeping giant yet to be awakened from the passive slumber brought on almost seventeen centuries ago. There have been times of renewal and revival which intermittently touched the history of Christianity, but, for the most part, the vigor of disciplemaking and every believer actively ministering to proclaim the gospel and edify the Body of Christ, has not been reclaimed.

## EQUIPPING: MINISTRY FUNCTION

A biblical solution to this dilemma can be found in the inspired writings of Paul, "And he gave some, apostles; and some, prophets; and some, evangelists; and some, pastors and teachers; For the perfecting of the saints, for the work of the ministry, for the edifying of the body of Christ: Till we all come in the unity of the faith, and of the knowledge of the Son of God, unto a perfect man, unto the measure of the stature of the fullness of Christ" (Ephesians 4:11-13).

The work of the ministry offices are described here. We will focus on the work of the pastor/teacher since it is most crucial for the local church development as we experience ministry today.

Each of these three verses, it seems, deal with a component of ministry. Verse 11 gives the ministry offices. Verse 12, it seems, speaks about ministry functions. Verse 13 describes the ultimate ministry goal, "the fullness of Christ." Logical deduction would lead to an interpretation where the ministry offices perform the ministry functions in order to reach the ministry goal. That would seem to be the simplest interpretation of this passage. Yet that is not the case. Subscribing to this view places the responsibility of ministry solely on the ministry offices and allows the laity to remain passive. The clergy-laity split continues if this interpretation is held.

The correct interpretation of Paul's writing here issues the primary call for the pastor/teacher to be equipping the saints for the work of ministry.[64] As the saints join the ministry in doing the work of ministering, the wonderful phenomena of the edifying of the Body of Christ takes form. It is in the context of equipping believers and full participation in ministering that edification results and the ministry goal of the "fullness of Christ" is achieved. Responsibility for ministering is not reserved for the elite professional clergy in this passage. It is to be shared with all believers when they have been equipped through the guidance of the pastor/teacher.

Here, then, is a crucial link to enable the body to do the work of Christ. Every member must be mobilized for the work of ministry. According to Ephesians, the role of the pastor/teacher is to equip (perfect) the members of the Body to the extent that they are prepared to do the work of the ministry as God leads them in their cities and neighborhoods.

What a beautiful sight to see churches where the laity are prepared and enthused in their call to join the pastor/teacher in doing the work of the ministry. The sleeping giant is the laity. The Body will not be able to do the work of Christ without enlisting this massive work force. Christ intended no other strategy. This is one of the great keys to the success of the primitive Church. "The success of any organization is in direct proportion to its ability to mobilize every participant in achieving its goal."[65] They successfully saw the laity motivated by the gospel, equipped by the disciplemaking communities, and empowered by the Holy Spirit.

The "equipping" mentioned here closely resembles the "committing" Paul mentioned to Timothy, as well as the work of Christ with the twelve, in "discipling." Each of these calls activate the believers to advance the kingdom of God and to minister one to another in word and deed. Whether "committing," "equipping," or "disciplemaking," contemporary ministry must come to the realization that we need to imitate Christ.

## GIFTS OF GRACE

**Objective:** The individual will demonstrate an understanding of the processes of spiritual formation through *gifts of grace* by listing and describing the grace gifts.

Unless you become involved in the activities of your church, you will never truly feel satisfied with that church.[66]

## INVOLVEMENT

It is the nature of people to want to be involved. Everyone likes to have the inner question, "Am I valuable?" answered affirmatively. One of the most effective tools of assimilation is the ability to plug new converts into tasks and roles at the church that give them significance immediately. These opportunities need to be valid roles which are needful, though they may be filled by someone with little prior experience around the church. The best use of this tool is when the task fits naturally with the interests of the person. It is best when they aim toward meeting needs or extending love and care.

Entry-level opportunities may come from every area of church life whether in the sanctuary, in various ministries, around the building, on the grounds, to the community, or through one's personal life. It is a church which is sensitive to new converts' needs and lay involvement that is constantly looking for new opportunities for involvement. Also, the members of a church need to be educated in the benefits of enlisting new believers. There have been churches where it was very difficult to break through certain barriers and finally be given a task or position. Every ministry of the local church should be alerted to the need for finding involvement opportunities for all.

Win Arn has found that churches that are growing and healthy offer sixty tasks or roles to every one hundred adults. The church that is plateaued only offers forty-three, in comparison. And the church that is in a state of decline offers approximately twenty-seven tasks or roles per one hundred adults.[67] It is clear to see the importance of involving people, both new and old, in the activities and ministries of a congregation.

## GRACE GIFTS

Using people according to their spiritual gifting is a key to participation assimilation. The grace gifts of Romans 12:4-9, it seems, are the most applicable since they are described as resident gifts flowing from the grace that is in the believer. Romans teaches that believers may be graced and gifted as teachers, leaders, servers, or givers. Ephesians 4 speaks of the ministry gifts which come through specific callings of the

Lord, such as apostle, prophet, evangelist, pastor, or teacher. First Corinthians 12 teaches about the manifestation gifts which are clearly demonstrated as the Spirit desires at His time. These are gifts of the Spirit such as healing, faith, miracles, wisdom, or discernment. The grace gifts, in contrast, it seems, are planted in the life of the believer, and through maturation and cultivation they will work to edify the Body.

Believers should be taught to seek to understand this grace that God has given them so that they can nurture it and minister most effectively. As they become familiar with the gifts, they will also see how they personally fit into the congregation's overall ministry as well as understand the place and role of others. Elmer Towns writes that believers who are working in their gifting are *happy*, because they get pleasure operating in their gift. They are *energized* because they get strength from their gifting. They are *productive* because they are effective in their gift. They will *sacrifice* because there is willingness and singleness of spirit. And they are more *spiritual* because they are in tune with the Spirit who is empowering them. For satisfied workers and new converts there is great benefit to helping each find a place of service in their gifting.[68]

## MOBILIZATION

Clearly a vital need for outreach and evangelism is motivating the believers, new and old, to involvement in ministry. Howard Butt said, "We have developed a spectator Christianity in which few speak and many listen. The New Testament Church commenced with Jesus saying to every one of His followers, apostles, and ordinary believers alike, 'Go ye into all the world and preach the gospel.' These words were not spoken in a pastor's conference or a seminary classroom. They were spoken to all His disciples. But what started as a lay movement has deteriorated into a professional pulpitism financed by lay spectators."[69]

Acts 8:4 shows this New Testament Church pattern, "Therefore they that were scattered abroad went everywhere preaching the Word." Perhaps some might suggest that it was the apostles, or those who were called into specific ministries, who really went everywhere. But certainly there were more than twelve who were instrumental in "turning the world upside down." Even if we consider all the good deacons modeled after Stephen's ministry, or the evangelists such as

Philip who went to Samaria, we will not be able to explain the world-shaking movement of the Early Church evangelism. Certainly it was a movement where every participant helped spread the message of Christ and His gospel.

## LAY MOVEMENT

No, this amazing growth of the Church in the first three centuries cannot be described in terms of ministry only. Acts 8:1 shows the context of this discussion and states, "All were scattered abroad. . . except the apostles." Sure, some ministry people were involved, but the mass exodus from the Jerusalem area included far more laity escaping the persecution of believers than the Church leaders. And as they went, they proclaimed the "good news." They had been transformed by this life and could not keep themselves from telling others about this Messiah. They established new homes all through the region and witnessed of the gospel and power of Christ. The same zeal that had shaken Jerusalem spread their faith through villages, towns, cities, and yes, "turned the world upside down."

The laity had been mobilized, and the impact is still awe-inspiring today. A Christian apologist of the second century would write, "We are everywhere. We are in your towns and in your cities; we are in your country; we are in your army and navy; we are in your palaces; we are in the senate; we are more numerous than anyone."[70] This was, and is, God's divine plan. Each believer filled with the life of Christ becomes an ambassador for the new kingdom. Only as churches provide opportunities for participation will new converts feel this mandate to unite and identify with the advance of God's work in the world.

## OPTIONAL GIFTS?

The amazing truth is that God has given gifts to His people so that they can carry out His Great Commission. That is exactly what the Word says, "Wherefore he saith, When he ascended up on high, he led captivity captive, *and gave gifts unto men*" (Ephesians 4:8). When God gives a gift, it is significant. I have gifts that I have never used stacked away in a closet or drawer. But when God gives a gift, it is necessary, not optional. His gifts edify the church, empower individuals, and fulfill His will in the earth. That sounds relatively significant to me.

## BELIEVER BENEFITS

Look what the working of the grace gifts can do for the believers:

1. It will assist them in knowing God's will for their lives.
2. It is similar to finding one's spiritual job description.
3. It enables them to take their appropriate places in the Body.
4. It helps them to see themselves as channels of God's grace.
5. It will help avoid "weariness in well doing" and burnout.
6. It brings greater understanding and appreciation for what others in the Body are called and anointed to do.
7. It emphasizes the need for unity of the Spirit in the Body.
8. It motivates them toward the true purpose of the Church.
9. It increases lay involvement in ministry.
10. It satisfies, energizes, and in every way brings out the best in the lives of the believers.[71]

## BODY BENEFITS

In addition to these wonderful benefits for every believer, the Body is edified in a particularly beautiful way when the grace gifts of God are flourishing. I like to describe it by imagining how a church, complete with all the grace gifts operative, would minister. Suppose the object of ministry was a homeless street person. How would God energize ministry in each one of these grace gifts?

### Prophecy

Romans 12:6-8 begins with the grace gift of prophecy. If a person graced with this gifting were to drive down the road and see a street person, what would he do? Note, this is not like the prophets of the Old Testament or the New Testament, but a person with the grace of sensing and ministering to things from a prophetic perspective. It is important to note that prophets are sensitive to sin and its influence. His reaction would be to feel a strong desire to expose the sin in this man's life that was destroying him. He would say that man was on the street because he had let sin destroy him and needed to repent so that God could put his life back together again through grace. This would be the ministry of grace working through a "prophet."

## Ministry

If one of the church members graced with ministry, or service, drove by this man, he would be touched with the need to help him. Most likely he would rush home and quickly fill a couple of grocery bags with supplies and go give them to him. The motivation would be to meet the need quickly and personally. The grace of ministry and service can be a wonderful strength to a congregation.

## Teaching

A member who had the grace gift of teaching would react differently. His motivation is to instruct so that people can live better lives for God. He might possibly go and research all the facts concerning help for street people in the region. Then he would go to the man and teach him about the churches that offer soup lines or meals on certain days, or the places where he could find temporary lodging. He would give him all the information he could share as to how to survive and even overcome this sad situation. For the teacher, providing instruction and information, it seems, is the most logical way to help this man recover.

## Exhortation

The exhorter is stirred by the awesome potential in every person. Looking at this man, he would see the wasted life. He would sense the need to challenge the man to reform his life and recover the God-given potential he had for life. He would "exhort" him to be all he could be rather than waste his life, health, and relationships in the life of the street. Usually an exhorter will give simple logical steps to accomplish the needed transformation. He is motivated to help people to achieve their best.

## Giving

Some people think that givers need to be wealthy, but this is not always the case. A giver has been given the grace gift of recognizing resources that others may not be able to see. The giver might not stop immediately to help this man on the street, nor will he always give of his own means. Rather, he would tap resources available to him to try to supply the need. This man might go to a grocer friend and ask for a donation, or to other contacts. One giver friend of mine buys scrap and junk which he redeems for cash and gives from that supply. He is not rich, but he gives proportionately much greater than others with similar income.

## Ruling

The ruler has the grace of administration or leadership. His reaction is different as well. He will probably never contact the man on the street personally. But the burden will touch him, and his gift will motivate him to action. He will begin to get a vision of how the entire problem of street people in the city can be solved. He will share the idea, motivate others to join him, and finally, structure a ministry to help people such as this in their need. Grace-gifted leaders see the big picture.

## Mercy

Finally, the person graced with mercy is full of the grace of compassion. He will feel so strongly for the individual personally that he will possibly stop the car immediately and go to this man. He is moved by the need, certainly, but in a different way from the server or giver. His feeling is more focused on the man personally and his sense of despair and rejection. His response is less to the natural need and more to the emotional need of the man. Symbolically I suggest that he will come to the man, put his arm around him, giving love and identifying with his hurt. He is the one who wants to walk with him in his shoes and feel his pain.

## HOLISTIC MINISTRY

When all of these are operative in a congregation and in balance, God has supplied a holistic full-ministry team to work with any type of need that may occur. Balance comes as we all understand one another's ministry gifts as well as our own. Then we realize how our ministry will benefit and what another's can do in other ways. We see ourselves as a part of the Body ministering with other parts to fulfill the needs. We are satisfied, we understand and complement others, and we all work together to edify the Body.

# COMMUNITY

**Objective:** The individual will demonstrate an understanding of the process of spiritual formation through *community* by discussing the "one another" passages.

## COMMUNITY REFLECTING CHRIST

"The church that preaches the gospel must embody the gospel. The good news must be seen in our corporate relationships, worship, joy, and life. With the steady erosion of relationships in today's world, the church needs urgently to become a visible community marked by love, God's new society in Christ."[72]

Great advances have been made through great preachers and ministers, but these will not be the vehicle for the culmination of Christ's work on earth. It is for the Church to come to reflect His person before a world of darkness.

"Jesus said he would create something else on the earth, something even more majestic than the mountains, something that would shine brighter than the stars. Something that would provide even more powerful evidence of His presence in the world. 'I will build my church,' He said, 'and the gates of hell shall not prevail against it.' . . .The church. . .bodies of believers assembled in local communities, is the only group of people with the potential to express God's character. . .Only the church. . .who loves Him and loves one another, can express His nature to a world hungry for reality."[73]

"One of the great unresolved challenges facing us as God's people today is to discover how to be true community in this transient, on-the-run society of ours."[74] The New Testament provides important keys toward this discovery in the life and ministry of Jesus, and later in the example of the primitive Church communities.

## JESUS AND COMMUNITY RELATING

In Jesus' relationships with His twelve, we can find a model for our lives and ministries today. Jesus understood and used the power of community and relating to anchor these men as the foundation of His Church. Community relating was not new or strange to the Lord as He chose His disciples.

Though Christ has been pictured as a loner, this is far from the truth. His very existence for eternity demonstrates the miracle and mandate of relating. From eternity Christ had been in relationship with the Father and the Holy Spirit. As the second Person of the trinity, the Word, He is personal for all time. An impersonal God cannot relate. The capacity for relationship is nonexistent. Christ is personal by His very nature and existence in the Godhead.

His nature did not change through the incarnation. Christ continued to be a personal Saviour and Lord. Though He was indeed God made flesh, He was always connected in relationship with the Father and the Holy Spirit, as well as with those He called. For this reason His ministry was marked, not by domineering dictatorship as in the legends of the Greek gods, but by a yielded dependence on the Father as He ministered in the flesh. John 8:28 demonstrates this, "Then said Jesus unto them, When ye have lifted up the Son of man, then shall ye know that I am he, and that I do nothing of myself; but as my Father hath taught me, I speak these things." Many other times in the Gospels this idea is repeated clearly to show Christ's connection and dependence on the Father, even though He was the Son of God (John 6:57; 8:16, 19, 28, 29; 5:17, 19, 26, 30, 36, 37). Jesus lived and moved in relationship.

In the Old Testament, relating is shown through God's dealing with the people of Israel. God called this people to Himself. God revealed His desire that He would enter into relationship with His fallen creation. Hebrews 8:10 bears this out, "For this is the covenant that I will make with the house of Israel after those days, saith the Lord; I will put my laws into their mind, and write them in their hearts: and I will be to them a God, and they shall be to me a people." Throughout the revelation of God in Scripture is seen that God is reaching out to establish rapport with those that will come to Him. He seeks to reconcile men into an eternal relationship with Himself.

The Body of Christ is called to reflect the image of Christ to the world. To a great extent that means our relating in the Church is to be patterned after the relating of the Godhead in the Trinity. We are bound together as one in the Body. Though we are distinct members of the Body, we are incorporated as one. Our distinctions are still present and functional, yet our unity overwhelms them so that we are known as one. This is quite different from the popular Western mentality of individualism and distinctiveness that supersedes any connectedness or unity. The Body is designed for distinctive members with their functions while it miraculously fits them all together in a wonderful cooperative unity.

In the New Testament we do see individuals mightily used of God. Paul certainly was one of those. He was anointed for his mission and directed by the Holy Spirit. At the same time he was not an individual operating outside any boundaries of community or relationship. Paul was sent by a community of believers following the leadership of the Holy Spirit at Antioch. Also, as Paul traveled in ministry, he connected himself to the communities of faith which were born. His relations with these communities were intimate and strong as the pages of his epistles so powerfully relate.

The Bible shows that the seed for our understanding of community in the Body of Christ rests in the nature of Christ, personal deity constantly in communion with the Father and His Body. To be the Body of Christ doing His work, we will need to more fully understand the function of community and relationship. The popular scriptural illustration which represents the Church as a fold does not deal with the relational aspect. There the congregation is seen only as a gathering point for the maintenance of those in the shepherd's care. The illustration of the fold is not meant to describe the more active view of the congregation as a relating ministering entity in itself. It is the model of Jesus, His inherent relational character and His intimate discipling ministry with the twelve, which illumines the potential of community for the Church. The qualities necessary for such potential will be described more fully in the next few sections.

## THE REALITY OF TOGETHERNESS AND BROTHERLY LOVE

Tertullian relates the second-century witness of the pagans who said, "See how these Christians love one another!"[75]

The Church on the pages of the New Testament was committed to being a Body knit together by the common bond of Christ and His gospel. This is seen most radically in the book of Acts, yet it is born out through the epistles, particularly in the admonition passages. One phrase that describes this togetherness of the people of God is the usage of "one another." When this construct is studied, it paints a clear picture of the New Testament expectation for maximum relating one with another in the Church. Observe the list below which is not exhaustive:

- "Be devoted to one another in brotherly love" (Romans 12:10).
- "Accept one another" (Romans 15:7).
- "Live in harmony with one another" (Romans 12:16).
- "Instruct one another" (Romans 15:14).
- "Greet one another" (Romans 16:16).
- "Wait for each other" (1 Corinthians 11:33).
- "Have concern for each other" (1 Corinthians 12:25).
- "Serve one another in love" (Galatians 5:13).
- "Carry each other's burdens" (Galatians 6:2).
- "Encourage one another" (1 Thessalonians 5:11).
- "Live in peace with each other" (1 Thessalonians 5:13).
- "Be kind to each other" (1 Thessalonians 5:15).
- "Bearing with one another in love" (Ephesians 4:2).
- "Be kind and compassionate to one another, forgiving each other" (Ephesians 4:32).
- "Submit to one another" (Ephesians 5:21).
- "Bear with each other and forgive" (Colossians 3:13).
- "Confess your sins to each other and pray for each other" (James 5:16).
- "Love one another deeply, from the heart" (1 Peter 1:22).
- "Offer hospitality to one another" (1 Peter 4:9).
- "Clothe yourselves with humility toward one another" (1 Peter 5:5).
- "Fellowship with one another" (1 John 1:7).

If these texts suggest anything, it is that the Church Jesus Christ established was conscious of being a community before God, a community that belongs together, whose members are responsible for one another and have a common history in the salvation journey. We take for granted our nice but anonymous churches, well administered but largely without togetherness or familial love, and perhaps even assume that this is God's will. We no longer even notice how elementary requirements of New Testament life, mentioned above, do not occur in our practice of church. "It is not our guilt and failure that are really dangerous. The real danger comes from the fact that we are no longer even aware that we fall short of what community and people of God are, according to the New Testament, supposed to be."[76]

Francis Schaeffer said, ". . .let us have community within the church which includes all of life, and all of life's needs — including the material needs. . .There are to be the kinds of human relationships that are necessary to show community within our groups, to give what humanism longs for and cannot produce. . .People are looking at us. . .to produce something that will bring the world to a standstill — human beings treating human beings like human beings. . .The church will not stand in our generation, the church will not be a striking force in our generation unless. . .it keeps the strength of the Christian dogmas and at the same time produces communities with beauty as well as truth."[77]

Finally, John 13:34, 35 and 17:21 affirm what Ephesians was leading us to understand. True outreach in the Spirit and character of Christ is debilitated without the interior treasures of love and unity. "A new commandment I give unto you, That ye love one another; as I have loved you, that ye also love one another. By this shall all men know that ye are my disciples, if ye have love one to another." Add to this the Lord's prayer to the Father, "That they all may be one; as thou, Father, art in me, and I in thee, that they also may be one in us: that the world may believe that thou hast sent me."

The Church stands out distinctively by its call to be the one place, in this world filled with broken relationships, where anyone can find "belonging." Joseph Tosini says, "Evidence is overwhelming that the deepest desire of the human heart is for relationships. . .People not only have an innate need for relationships, God also planted in us a compelling desire for permanency in those relationships — another facet of the eternity He has set in our hearts. . .A person's greatest joy and deepest sorrow are rooted in relationships. This need for relationship is the continuing theme of the Bible. . .It can be a great relief to find that our highest calling is simply to pursue what is in God's heart: family. We all receive that calling. It's the call to be rightly related to God and to one another."[78]

## SPIRITUAL WARFARE

**Objective:** The individual will demonstrate an understanding of the processes of spiritual formation in *spiritual warfare* by describing the authority believers have over principalities and powers.

Luke writes, "And the seventy returned again with joy, saying, Lord, even the devils are subject unto us through thy name. And he said unto them, I beheld Satan as lightning fall from heaven. Behold, I give unto you power to tread on serpents and scorpions, and over all the power of the enemy: and nothing shall by any means hurt you" (Luke 10:17-19).

It is interesting to observe that the disciples realized that the devils were subject unto them through the name of Jesus. These men had not as yet received the baptism of the Holy Spirit. Jesus was not yet ascended. Calvary had not yet passed. But their lives with Christ and their faith in Him was effective against the devils. Certainly this passage is given to believers to anchor their confidence that the children of God have power over the enemy. We do not have to be fearful concerning his apparent powers or destruction. By the name of Jesus, His eternal Word, and the blood of the Lamb of God, we can stand boldly against his attacks.

Another interesting observation is that immediately after the remark by the disciples, Jesus speaks of Satan's fall. Though we often fail to quote this verse in connection with our power in Christ, the connection is clear. Satan has been cast out of heaven. He is a created being made by the hand of God. Though he is mighty and clever, he is not, nor could he ever come close to being, God. He is not omnipotent, omniscient, or omnipresent. He was defeated from heaven before, he was defeated on Calvary later, and he will one day be ultimately defeated and thrown into the lake of fire. Our Savior has defeated him repeatedly.

Next, Jesus teaches the disciples that He has given them power. This is our place today. We are God's children, living in His name, covered by His blood, standing on the promises of His Word. We have power to defeat Satan. The word that Luke wrote to speak of Satan's power is *dunamis,* which refers to might or force and is commonly used in the New Testament (Acts 1:8). When He speaks of the gift of power for believers, He uses the word *exousia,* which speaks of authority or control, as a magistrate or potentate might have. Though Satan does generate an appearance of awesome power, we have something more. We have been given delegated authority from the King of Kings over Satan and all his devils.

In spite of the fact that Satan seems so powerful in his destruction and darkness through society, we have this promise from the Word of God. Jesus has defeated Satan, and now He has given to us the right or privilege to represent His authority over all Satan's darkness. It does not matter how powerful Satan may appear to us. We know that we are charged with authority by the One who has repeatedly defeated him.

Imagine that an eighteen-wheeler was rolling down the road. And suppose that a skinny little state patrol officer stepped out onto the pavement and held up his hand. Now who has more power? more weight? more force? The truck, of course. But what do you think will happen? The truck stops because the skinny little patrolman has authority delegated to him from the government of the state. The entire law enforcement department of the state, all of the legal system with its laws, and the citizens as a whole are represented by this one skinny little patrolman. The truck driver knows that his power is no match for the authority which this patrolman represents. The same is true of our authority as representatives of Christ.

A story has been told about the only American general taken captive in World War II. The news came through underground sources that the war was over and that the allies had defeated Germany. The general limped on his cane into the office of the commander of the prisoner-of-war camp. He pointed his cane at the man who had ordered cruelty and pain on the prisoners, and he said, "My commander and chief has defeated your commander and chief, and I am taking charge of this camp." When we feel like Satan is crowding us too close we can tell him the same thing.

## DECEPTION

One of the most important things to know when we stand against the enemy is that he has no authority. He has to fight with the only weapon that he has left, deception. It would be similar to a huge old lion that had lost all of his claws and his teeth. He still looks terrifying. He still sounds terrifying. He could scare anyone into a heart attack who didn't realize his condition. But he is harmless. He has no weapon.

When Jesus died for us on the cross, he defeated Satan and took back from him the weapon he had been using for centuries — the deed, so to speak. Look at Scripture: "And you, being dead in your sins and the uncircumcision of your flesh, hath he quickened together with him, having forgiven you all trespasses; Blotting out the handwriting of ordinances that was against us, which was contrary to us, and took it out of the way, nailing it to his cross; And having spoiled principalities and powers, he made a shew of them openly, triumphing over them in it" (Colossians 2:13-15).

There on the cross Christ not only paid the price for our sins, but also erased a horrible decree that was against us all. At the creation Adam had been given dominion over the earth by God. In effect he had the title deed to the earth. When he fell, he surrendered the dominion he once had to Satan. All mankind came under the curse of sin. Till the cross, Satan had held this legal dominion. God had rightly given it to Adam, and he had tragically lost it.

The message of this passage is victorious. Jesus blotted out the ordinance. We can understand now how it was against us and contrary to us, since it went against everything for which God had created man. There at Calvary Jesus took it out of the way and nailed it to the cross. He covered it and Satan lost that authority over creation which he had stolen and enjoyed since the fall.

Now the only weapon left him is deception. That is what he used in the garden, and since the cross he has had to rely on it again. This is the message believers need to understand. If Adam and Eve had not yielded to the subtle deceiving lies of the serpent, Satan would have had no power over them. They gave him power by responding. The same is true since the cross. Only when people believe his deceiving lies, intimidation, fear tactics, subtle influence, illusions, alluring, or such tricks can he gain any power.

There are several lessons in this for us as we wage war against this doomed foe: Satan has no real authority over us as believers; We give him power when we yield to his enticements or lies; He has learned how to deceive man very effectively; We have true authority over him and his devils; Our victory has been won and his doom sealed.

**PRAYER**

The Bible teaches us that "the weapons of our warfare are not carnal, but mighty through God to the pulling down of strong holds" (2 Corinthians 10:4). It also allows us to understand that we are not fighting "against flesh and blood, but against principalities, against powers, against the rulers of the darkness of this world, against spiritual wickedness in high places" (Ephesians 6:12). Knowing this, the truth becomes apparent that the prayer of faith is one of the greatest weapons against the enemy. As believers pray, the strength of heaven is focused against the enemy to defeat his works.

One of the true marks of a time of revival and evangelism is prayer. Here at the end of the century renewed interest in prayer has seen a marked increase. Many of the fastest-growing churches in the world have built strong ministries of prayer. Dr. Paul Yongi Cho, pastor of the largest church in the world (Seoul, Korea), commits himself to three to five hours of prayer daily. The nation of Korea has seen tremendous advances in evangelical ministries because of prayer. Since the Korean war the nation has experienced a prolonged commitment to massive prayer.

Commonly, in the early morning hours large numbers of believers go to the hills to pray. This writer experienced this firsthand on a visit to Seoul. The first morning we were surprised to hear the voices of many believers praying out in the countryside. It was evident that this was a habitual practice well ingrained through the years. Certainly this is the reason Korea has become the nation with the greatest growth in evangelism. It is now thought of as the greatest Christian nation per capita. Korea has become a great missionary-sending nation because of this revival of prayer.

If prayer is indeed the mightiest weapon of spiritual war, then God surely is raising an army for His last days. Many different movements of prayer are springing up over the world, motivating believers to come together and pray. As ministers, leaders, or laymen we have a call from heaven to join the army of God uniting in prayer to defeat the foe and claim ground for our King.

## FAITH

**Objective:** The individual will demonstrate an understanding of the processes of spiritual formation through *faith* by identifying the source of faith.

### FAITH DEFINED

"Now faith is the substance of things hoped for, the evidence of things not seen" (Hebrews 11:1). In this passage God is giving the definition of faith. The NRSV translates,

"Now faith is the assurance of things hoped for, the conviction of things not seen." The NIV says, "Now faith is being sure of what we hope for and certain of what we do not see."

Moffatt's translation of this verse reads, "Now faith means that we are confident of what we hope for, convinced of what we do not see." Another translation says, "Faith is giving substance to things hoped for." Another reads, "Faith is the warranty deed, the thing for which we have hoped is at last ours." Still another adds, "Faith is grasping the unrealities of hope and bringing them into the realm of reality."[79]

The word "substance" from this verse is used four other times in the New Testament. Three times it is translated with a form of "confidence." The other time it is translated with the word "person," referring to the person of Christ (Hebrews 1:3). This is a composite word which unites the two thoughts "to stand" and "under." Faith is described then as that which stands under, a setting under or support, establishing the thing hoped for. The confident faith of believers stands in anticipation and makes space for the reality coming.

The word "evidence" is to convince, prove, or convict. In this second phrase of the verse, faith is described as "the proof of things hoped for." Faith is rightly said to be the "warranty deed" of what is hoped for. There is clear indication from this verse of Scripture that faith is the substance of those things desired until the reality appears. This faith actually moves beyond hope to become an active expectation of the coming reality. Hope longs for the thing while faith anticipates and acts as though it is at the door.

## SOURCE OF FAITH

Where does faith come from? How can faith be increased? The Word says "Faith comes by hearing, and hearing by the word of God" (Romans 10:17). Since this is true, faith is increased as believers fill their lives with the Word. This is quite revealing because it exposes the opposite truth. The reason believers have so little faith to exercise is the lack of the Word of God filling their lives. The application from these thoughts is, that the more Christians exercise themselves in Scripture the more their faith will grow.

There is one disclaimer to this application. Some believers make it a ritual to read the Bible, some even memorize it, but their faith doesn't seem to grow. Does this nullify the truth that the Word of God brings faith? No. The Bible says it is "not of the letter, but of the Spirit: for the letter killeth, but the Spirit giveth life" (2 Corinthians 3:6). It also adds, "It is the spirit that quickeneth; the flesh profiteth nothing: the words that I speak unto you, they are spirit, and they are life" (John 6:63).

Exercising oneself in the Scripture without the illumination of the Spirit is less effective, or the Bible says ineffective, to increase faith. Two Greek words are often translated as the Word in the Bible, *logos* and *rhema*. *Logos* speaks of the expression of God and is used in John 1:1 saying, "In the beginning was the Word." It refers there to Jesus, or to the whole counsel of God elsewhere. *Rhema* is often used to speak of a particular passage of Scripture that is illumined by the Spirit for a specific application. Some have called it a word from the Word. With this in mind, it would be a *rhema* from the *logos* that the Spirit would use to build faith.

Believers who experience faith rising as they engage in God's Word are usually inspired by the Spirit in a particular passage which specifically speaks to illuminate their situation. That is a *rhema* from God's *logos,* a word quickened by the Spirit from the Word of God. So what should Christians do, wait with their Bible in hand till the Spirit inspires them? No. Believers should search the Scriptures for passages which speak accurately and directly to their need or situation. By meditating on these sections of Holy Scripture they are filling their minds, hearts, and spirits with God's thoughts, His Word. As they work with the Word, searching it and applying it in this way, the Spirit will illumine some portion and faith will come forth. Rather than waiting passively and praying for faith, believers can dive into God's promises and then experience the Spirit bringing light to their needs and faith to their hearts. Believers who understand this begin to stand up and say, "God's Word says it, and I am believing it to happen."

**Faith vs. Feelings.** When believers have gone through the process above, often they are so confident in their faith in God's Word that they begin to praise Him for what they know will come to pass. To some that sounds strange, praising God for what has not happened yet. Many would say, "But what if it doesn't happen?" Think about that statement. Isn't that doubt? Who would give us such a thought? How often

Christians don't even discern what forces are influencing their thoughts and actions.

God has said in His Word that His children are to walk by faith, not by their senses (2 Corinthians 5:7). Smith Wigglesworth once said, "I can't understand God by feelings. I can't understand the Lord Jesus Christ by feelings. I can only understand God the Father and Jesus Christ by what the Word says about them. God is everything the Word says He is. We need to get more acquainted with Him through the Word."[80]

Again, walking by faith means walking by the Word of God, not by our feelings and the surrounding circumstances. Everyone knows that emotions are volatile and fickle, but God's Word never changes. The thoughts of men and situations often change, yet God's Word remains the same. This is the cornerstone of our faith.

**Faith Means Action.** One quick reading through the Bible confirms that faith is active, not passive. Peter believed it was Christ on the water, so he responded, acted, and got out of the boat. Look at other Bible leaders, and you will see the same. Faith is seeing what God wants done and moving to be His tool to see it accomplished.

# Spiritual Formation
# Through Disciplines
# Unit Two

# Objective:

The individual will demonstrate an understanding of the process of spiritual formation through various *disciplines.*

**Disciplines:**
Prayer
Fasting
Meditation
Study
Journaling
Confession
Solitude
Service

## PRAYER

**Objective:** The individual will demonstrate an understanding of the processes of spiritual formation through *prayer* by listing prayer models.

*Richard Foster,* Celebration of Discipline, *pp. 33-45*

Real prayer is life-creating and life-changing. "Prayer — secret, fervent, believing prayer — lies at the root of all godliness,"[81] writes William Carey. To pray is to change. Prayer is the central avenue God uses to transform us. If we are unwilling to change, we will abandon prayer as a noticeable characteristic of our lives. The closer we come to the heartbeat of God, the more we see our need and the more we desire to be conformed to Christ. William Blake tells us that our task in life is to learn to bear God's "beams of love." How

often we fashion cloaks of evasion — beam-proof shelters —
in order to elude our eternal Lover. But when we pray, God
slowly and graciously reveals to us our evasive actions and
sets us free from them.

## MODELS

All who have walked with God have viewed prayer as the
main business of their lives. The words of the Gospel of Mark,
"And in the morning, a great while before day, he rose and
went out to a lonely place, and there he prayed," stand as a
commentary on the lifestyle of Jesus (Mark 1:35). [Note also
David, the apostles, and others.] Martin Luther declares, "I
have so much business I cannot get on without spending
three hours daily in prayer." He held it as a spiritual axiom
that "he that has prayed well has studied well."[82] John Wesley
said, "God does nothing but in answer to prayer,"[83] and
backed up his conviction by devoting two hours daily to that
sacred exercise. The most notable feature of David Brainerd's
life was his praying. His journal is permeated with accounts
of prayer, fasting, and meditation. "I love to be alone in my
cottage, where I can spend much time in prayer. . .I set apart
this day for secret fasting and prayer to God."[84]

For those explorers in the frontiers of faith, prayer was no
little habit tacked onto the periphery of their lives; it was
their lives. It was the most serious work of their most productive years. William Penn testified of George Fox that,
"Above all he excelled in prayer. . .The most awful, living,
reverend frame I ever felt or beheld, I must say was his in
prayer."[85] Adoniram Judson sought to withdraw from business and company seven times a day in order to engage in
the holy work of prayer. He began at dawn, then at nine,
twelve, three, six, nine, and midnight he would give time to
secret prayer. John Hyde of India made prayer such a dominant characteristic of his life that he was nicknamed,
"Praying Hyde." For these, and all those who have braved the
depths of the interior life, to breathe was to pray.

## LEARNING TO PRAY

Real prayer is something we learn. The disciples asked
Jesus, "Lord, teach us to pray" (Luke 11:1). They had prayed
all their lives, and yet something about the quality and
quantity of Jesus' praying caused them to see how little they

knew about prayer. If their praying was to make any difference on the human scene, there were some things they needed to learn.

It was liberating to me to realize that prayer involved a learning process. I was set free to question, to experiment, even to fail, for I knew I was learning. For years I had prayed for many things, and with great intensity, but with only marginal success. But then I saw that I might possibly be doing some things wrong and could learn differently. I took the Gospels and cut out every reference to prayer and pasted them on to sheets of paper. When I could read Jesus' teachings on prayer in one sitting, I was shocked. Either the excuses and rationalizations for unanswered prayer I had been taught were wrong, or Jesus' words were wrong. I determined to learn to pray so that my experience conformed to the words of Jesus, rather than try to make His words conform to my experience.[86]

## COMMITTED TO PRAY

We must never wait until we feel like praying before we pray. Prayer is like any other work; we may not feel like working, but once we have been at it for a bit, we begin to feel like working. We may not feel like practicing the piano, but once we play for a while, we feel like doing it. In the same way, our prayer muscles must be limbered up a bit and once the blood-flow of intercession begins, we will find that we like praying.[87] We need not worry that this work will take up too much of our time, for "it takes no time, but it occupies all our time."[88] It is not prayer in addition to work, but prayer simultaneous with work. We precede, enfold, and follow all our work with prayer. Prayer and action become wedded.

Though in many ways we can see prayer as parallel to work, the work of the believer, in fact, it is a way of being with God and communing with Him. A commitment to prayer is more a commitment to meeting Him than a work ethic.

# FASTING

**Objective:** The individual will demonstrate an understanding of the processes of spiritual formation through *fasting* by listing common types of fasts.

*Donald S. Whitney*, Spiritual Disciplines for the Christian Life, *pp. 151, 152*

## DREADED

"Fasting is the most feared and misunderstood of all the spiritual disciplines. One reason fasting is feared is that many believe it turns us into something we don't want to become and causes things to happen that we don't want to happen. We fear that fasting will make us hollow-eyed fanatics or odd for God. We're afraid that it will make us suffer dreadfully and give us a generally negative experience.

For some Christians, fasting for spiritual purposes is as unthinkable as shaving their head or walking barefoot across a fire pit . . . .And yet it's mentioned in Scripture more times than even something as important as baptism (seventy-seven to seventy-five times mentioned). . . .To those unfamiliar with fasting, the most surprising part of this chapter may be the discovery that Jesus expected that His followers would fast. Notice Jesus' words at the beginning of Matthew 6:16, 17: "when you fast."

## DEFINED

A biblical definition of fasting is a Christian's voluntary abstinence from food for spiritual purposes. There is a broader view of fasting that is often overlooked. This is the approach Richard Foster takes when he defines fasting as "the voluntary denial of a normal function for the sake of intense spiritual activity."[89] So then, fasting does not always deal with abstinence from food. Sometimes we may need to fast from involvement with other people, or from the media, from the telephone, from talking, from sleep, etc., in order to become more absorbed in a time of spiritual activity . . . Strictly speaking, however, the Bible refers to fasting only in terms of its primary sense; that is, abstinence from food.

*Richard Foster, Celebration of Discipline, pp. 47-54.*

## DEADLY

Fasting has developed a bad reputation as a result of the excessive ascetic practices of the Middle Ages. With the decline of the inward reality of the Christian faith, an increasing tendency to stress the only thing left, the outward form, developed. And whenever there is a form devoid of spiritual power, law will take over because law always carries with it a sense of security and manipulative power. Hence, fasting was subjected to the most rigid regulations and practiced with extreme self-mortification and flagellation. Modern culture reacts strongly to these excesses and tends to confuse fasting with mortification.

It is sobering to realize that the very first statement Jesus made about fasting dealt with the question of motive (Matthew 6:16, 17). To use good things to our own ends is always the sign of false religion. How easy it is to take something like fasting and try to use it to get God to do what we want. At times there is such stress upon the blessings and the benefits of fasting that we would be tempted to believe that with a little fast we could have the world, including God, eating out of our hands.

## DESCRIPTIONS

*Normal Fast*—abstaining from food while drinking water. See Matthew 4:2 where Jesus went forty days without food. Nothing is said of water since it is unlikely a person could live without water for so long.

*Partial Fast*—limiting the diet in some way while not going without food totally. This is fasting since the principle is abstaining, giving up something.

*Absolute Fast*—abstaining from all food and even water. (Ezra 10:6; Esther 4:16; Acts 9:9).

*Supernatural Fast*—abstaining from food and water for an extended time as when Moses was in the presence of the Lord on Mount Sinai forty days and nights without food or water (Deuteronomy 9:9).

*Private Fast*—the fast Jesus taught where no one should be aware of our fasting (Matthew 6:16).

*Congregational Fast*—fasting with others, as when a church or group of people are called to fast at the same time for the same purpose (Acts 13:2).

*National Fast*—Be similar to the congregational fast, but involving a whole nation of people (Jonah 3:5-8).

*Regular Fast*—setting aside a time to fast regularly. John Wesley set one requirement for ordination that a man would fast twice a week.

*Occasional Fast*—prompted by the Spirit or circumstances (Matthew 9:15).

## DELIGHTS

There are many benefits which may be derived from the spiritual discipline of fasting: one identifies more closely with the life and suffering of the Savior; prayer is strengthened; closer communion is felt; guidance, empowering; release for the expression of grief, deliverance, and protection; full and true humbling in repentance; intercession for the work of God; ministry strength; temptation can be overcome; and worship and love for God is renewed.

## MEDITATION

**Objective:** The individual will demonstrate an understanding of the processes of spiritual formation through *meditation* by listing Scripture references which call believers to this activity.

### THINK ON THESE THINGS

"Finally, brethren, whatsoever things are true, whatsoever things are honest, whatsoever things are just, whatsoever things are pure, whatsoever things are lovely, whatsoever things are of good report; if there be any virtue, and if there be any praise, think on these things" (Philippians 4:8). The command is direct. Paul is admonishing the Philippian saints to set their minds. He realizes that the mind is a powerful tool that can be used for our good or can be used for our destruction. It takes discipline to restrict the mind from wandering into dangerous areas, and meditation is one way that this can be done.

### RENEW THE MIND

"I beseech you therefore, brethren, by the mercies of God, that ye present your bodies a living sacrifice, holy, acceptable unto God, which is your reasonable service. And be not conformed to this world: but be ye transformed by the renewing of your mind, that ye may prove what is that good, and acceptable, and perfect, will of God." (Romans 12:1, 2). Transformation comes by renewing the mind. Old destructive habits of thought can be replaced with new spiritual habits of thought. This can happen through devoting time to the discipline of meditation, as the inspired Word of God fills one's mind and life renewal takes place. God's ways will grow in the place where the ways of self and sin once held control.

### BREAD OF LIFE

Jeremiah 15:16 says, "Thy words were found, and I did eat them; and thy word was unto me the joy and rejoicing of mine heart: for I am called by thy name, O Lord God of hosts."

Job 23:12 says, "Neither have I gone back from the commandment of his lips; I have esteemed the words of his mouth more than my necessary food."

Jesus told Satan, "It is written, Man shall not live by bread alone, but by every word that proceedeth out of the mouth of God" (Matthew 4:4).

The symbolism of the Word being like food and meditation similar to the digestive process is rich with application. The most prominent is that meditation is parallel to the ruminating process. Meditating on scripture is like the food that goes into the stomach of a cow and is brought back later to be chewed again. By routinely thinking on the Scriptures, we extract nurture, which could not be obtained with mere surface observation.

## DELIGHT IN THE LORD

Psalms 1:2, 3 says, "But his delight is in the law of the Lord; and in his law doth he meditate day and night. And he shall be like a tree planted by the rivers of water, that bringeth forth his fruit in his season; his leaf also shall not wither; and whatsoever he doeth shall prosper." The promise from this passage is that our lives can become like the tree which is always fed by the river's water. Meditation works to bring this about. It changes us and our thought patterns and wills, into His way of thinking and seeing. This occurs as we actively discipline our minds to rest in the Word. If the Word is filling the mind, then the product of the life will be built on that base.

## WHEN TO MEDITATE

"And these words, which I command thee this day, shall be in thine heart: And thou shalt teach them diligently unto thy children, and shalt talk of them when thou sittest in thine house, and when thou walkest by the way, and when thou liest down, and when thou risest up" (Deuteronomy 6: 6, 7).

Even as early as Israel's time, the heart of those that followed the Lord were challenged to meditate on the Lord constantly. Notice how all-encompassing the guidelines of this scripture are. Meditate when you are in your house, and when you are out by the way, or when you lie down, and when you rise up. It is certainly clear that God intends the believer's mind to be on Him and His Word at all times.

## BENEFITS OF MEDITATION

"This book of the law shall not depart out of thy mouth; but thou shalt meditate therein day and night, that thou mayest observe to do according to all that is written therein: for then thou shalt make thy way prosperous, and then thou shalt have good success" (Joshua 1:8). This scripture reveals that God's Word should be in our mouths consistently and that there are benefits when we comply. Meditation aids obedience and obedience brings prosperity and success. Paul taught this principle to Timothy saying, "Meditate upon these things; give thyself wholly to them; that thy profiting may appear to all" (1 Timothy 4:15).

## WISDOM THROUGH MEDITATION

"O how love I thy law! it is my meditation all the day. Thou through thy commandments hast made me wiser than mine enemies: for they are ever with me. I have more understanding than all my teachers: for thy testimonies are my meditation. I understand more than the ancients, because I keep thy precepts" (Psalm 119: 97-100).

Meditation on scripture is the never-ending process of mining for the riches of eternal truth and revelation tucked away in God's Word. Memorizing a passage is a great help to meditation since it frees persons to work with the text no matter where they are or what they are doing. Meditation involves keen and persevering observation. Repetition of small phrases helps. Emphasizing each word often leads to illumination. Questioning is one of the greatest tools. Questions of observation, "What is the author saying?" or questions of interpretation, "What does the author mean?" or questions of application, "What am I to do?" all unlock meaning from the text.

Meditation also helps the scripture to sink down into the heart and soul, far beyond mental exercise. It is an avenue of filling one's life with God's thoughts, His principles, and, actually, His presence. Meditation allows the Word to transform.

## STUDY

**Objective:** The individual will demonstrate an understanding of the processes of spiritual formation through the discipline of *study* by describing guidelines for this practice.

"Study to shew thyself approved unto God, a workman that needeth not to be ashamed, rightly dividing the word of truth"

(2 Timothy 2:15). It is interesting to note that the word Paul uses here is not translated as "study" in any other use in the New Testament. It is translated as "being forward," or "endeavoring," or "being diligent," or "laboring." From these uses it is easy to see that the thrust of the word is not simply accumulation of knowledge. It is an admonition from Paul for godly fervency in rightly dividing the Word, seeking constantly the approval of God. Howard Hendricks asks three questions to help apply this verse: "Is God well pleased? Is the work well done? Is the Word well used?"

The discipline of study, then, is a call for something more than information-gathering. The Word is to be intensely studied, extremely scrutinized. But the goal is not factual; it is transformational. Genuine study must cause men to see themselves as they stand before God, to see society as it stands before God, and to see the people of God as they stand before both God and the society to which they minister.

This explains why, on one hand, believers must study the Word of God diligently and on the other, why they must keenly study the society where they have been placed. Only to study the Bible reveals its truth but fails to deliver this truth in a relevant manner. Only to study man brings no hope for deliverance and redemption. Paul was gifted in this balance of knowing God's revelation and searching each city for means of delivery relevant to that society.

The discipline of study is also important because the mind is shaped by the structures it feeds upon. "The ingrained habits of thought will conform to the order of the thing being studied. What we study determines the kind of habits that are being formed. . . .This is why the issue of television programming is so important. With innumerable murders being portrayed each evening on prime time TV, the repetition alone trains the inner mind in destructive thought patterns. . . .[This] is why Paul urges us to focus on things that are true, honorable, just, pure, lovely and gracious."[90]

"Finally, brethren, whatsoever things are true, whatsoever things are honest, whatsoever things are just, whatsoever things are pure, whatsoever things are lovely, whatsoever things are of good report; if there be any virtue, and if there be any praise, think on these things" (Philippians 4:8).

### GUIDELINES FOR STUDY

There are three intrinsic and three extrinsic aids that will enhance anyone's time who is interested in learning the art of studying.[91] The first intrinsic guide is to seek to understand what the author is saying; second, to seek to interpret what the author means. These are closely related; still, there is a difference, and misunderstanding occurs in this difference. Third, is to seek to evaluate what the author is saying. Do you agree or disagree with the author? And why is that the case? What is valid and what do you question in the presentation? This type of thinking heightens the effectiveness of study tremendously.

The extrinsic guidelines start with experience. All that a person is exposed to is channeled through prior experience. For instance, if a person were reaching for a cup of coffee and his last cup had spilled on his hand, burning him, he would be cautious because of this prior experience. Another man without such prior experience may not display any caution. Experience influences everything we receive.

Next, other books related to our studies inform us. It is good to study more than one writer in any area just as it is good to read more than one commentary when studying the Bible. No one expert has all the knowledge in a field. Finally, live discussion is a factor. Study is greatly enhanced when there is opportunity for live discussion. It is there people interact with one another and fine-tune the information gleaned through study. Without such dialogue, it is more difficult for study to produce real learning that is applicable to life experience.

## NON-WRITTEN STUDY

Study is not limited to books. As a matter of fact, the greater part of study is not oriented to books. As believers seeking to grow, much can be gleaned from alert observation in this world which God has made, inhabited by man He has formed. All around us are illustrations of His craft and design. Through this we can see something of Him — not everything, but certainly something.

There is a wealth of study for one who is aware of nature. Many realize the insights which can be gleaned by observing people. It is necessary to learn from studying groups of people, such as the people of God. Christians must be arduous students of society. Sensitivity to every mood and swing in society feeds Christianity's ministry to the lost. And how can believers reach the entire globe with the gospel unless they are students of the cultures that cover this sphere? Study is vital.

# JOURNALING

**Objective:** The individual will demonstrate an understanding of the processes of spiritual formation through *journaling* by discussing the benefits of this discipline.

> *Ronald S. Whitney*, Spiritual Disciplines for the Christian Life, *pp. 195-197*
>
> That there is a crying need for the recovery of the devotional life cannot be denied. If anything characterizes modern Protestantism, it is the absence of spiritual disciplines or spiritual exercises. Yet such disciplines form the core of the life of devotion. It is not an exaggeration to state that this is the lost dimension in modern Protestantism.[92]

More than almost any other discipline, journaling has a fascinating appeal with nearly all who hear about it. One reason is the way journaling blends biblical doctrine and daily living, like the confluence of two great rivers into one. And since each believer's journey down life's river involves bends and hazards previously unexplored by them on the way to the celestial city, something about journaling this journey appeals to the adventuresome spirit of Christian growth.

Although the practice of journaling is not commanded in Scripture, it is modeled. And God has blessed the use of journals since Bible times. A journal (a word usually synonymous with diary) is a book in which a person writes down various things. A Christian's journal is a place to record the works and ways of God in his life. One's journal can also include an account of daily events, a diary of personal relationships, a notebook of insights into Scripture, and a list of prayer requests. It is a place where spontaneous devotional thoughts or lengthy theological musings can be preserved. A journal is one of the best places for charting one's progress in other spiritual disciplines and for holding oneself accountable to his goals.

Woven through the fabric of entries and events are the colorful strands of one's reflections and feelings about them. How a person responds to these matters and how he interprets them from his own spiritual perspective are at the heart of journaling.

The Bible itself contains many examples of God-inspired journals. Many Psalms are records of David's personal spiritual journey with the Lord. We call the journal of Jeremiah's feelings about the fall of Jerusalem the book of Lamentations. As you read. . .think carefully about joining these and others of God's people who have taken up the penned discipline of journaling "for the purposes of godliness." Remember, the goal of becoming more like Jesus should be the main reason for beginning any spiritual discipline, including this one. With that fresh in mind, consider the words of the United Kingdom's Maurice Roberts about journaling:

> The logic of this practice is inevitable once men have felt the urge to become molded in heart and life to the pattern of Christ. No one will keep a record of his inward groans, fears, sins, experiences, providences and aspirations unless he is convinced of the value of the practice for his own spiritual progress. It was this very conviction which made it a common practice in earlier times. We suggest the practice should be revived and something needs to be said in its defense.[93]

One of the ways the progress or decline of the inner man can be noted through journaling is the observation of patterns in one's life he has not seen before. When I review my journal entries for a month, six months, a year, I see myself and events more objectively. I can analyze my thoughts and actions apart from the feelings I had at the time. From that perspective it's easier to observe whether I've made spiritual progress or have backslidden in a particular area.

Journaling is not a time for navel-gazing, however. Nor is it an excuse for becoming self-centered at the expense of a needy world. Writing on the Puritans and their relationship to society, Edmund S. Morgan cites an entry from the journal of a godly young man during an illness from which he died in the late 1600s. In it the young man evaluates whether he had shown sufficient love to others. Then, says Morgan, "The fact that many Puritans kept diaries of this kind helps to explain their pursuit of social virtue: diaries were the reckoning books in which they checked the assets and liabilities of their souls in faith. When they opened these books, they set down lapses of morality with appropriate repentance and balanced them against the evidences of faith. Cotton Mather made a point of having at least one good action to set down in his diary on every day of the week.[94]

Whitney goes on to explain that journaling can be of value in the following areas:

Help in self-understanding and evaluation, help in meditation, help in expressing thoughts and feelings to the Lord, help in remembering the Lord's work, help in creating and preserving a spiritual heritage, help in clarifying and articulating insights and impressions, help in monitoring goals and priorities, help in maintaining the other spiritual disciplines.[95]

## CONFESSION

**Objective:** The individual will demonstrate an understanding of the processes of spiritual formation through *confession* by identifying characteristics of the mentoring relationship.

*Paul D. Stanley and J. Robert Clinton,* Connecting: Learning How to Learn From Others

Thou therefore, my son, be strong in the grace that is in Christ Jesus. And the things that thou hast heard of me among many witnesses, the same commit thou to faithful men, who shall be able to teach others also (2 Timothy 2:1, 2).

Confession is the classic name for the spiritual discipline that has been practiced through the centuries. Today this long-standing discipline is best reflected by the term "mentoring." Confession has come to be limited to the catholic tradition of priestly confession and does not carry the relational aspects of the discipline.

Mentoring is popular at present. Its popularity attests to its potential usefulness for all kinds of leadership. It also speaks of the tremendous relational vacuum in an individualistic society and its accompanying lack of accountability. In *Habits of the Heart,* the authors see individualism as an American asset turned into a liability. Americans cling to personal independence when they desperately need interdependence. But God did not create people to be self-sufficient and move through life alone. To return to healthy relational living will require recognition of this need and courage to change. In no other area is this change so urgently needed than in leadership development. Acknowledgement of this need is partially responsible for the groundswell toward mentoring. "Will you mentor me?" is being expressed in many ways in every area: business, ministry, family, military, education, and the church. This swelling cry for meaningful relationships can be a springboard to learning and growth.

Mentoring is a relational experience in which one person empowers another by sharing God-given resources. The following characteristics are helpful in forming such a relationship:

- Ability to readily see potential in a person.
- Tolerance with mistakes, brashness, abrasiveness, and the like in order to see that potential develop.
- Flexibility in responding to people and circumstances.
- Patience, knowing that time and experience are needed for development.
- Perspective, having vision and ability to see down the road and suggest the next steps that a mentoree needs.
- Gifts and abilities that build up and encourage others.

Barnabas was a people-influencer. He saw potential in Saul (later the apostle Paul) when others kept their distance. Saul's conversion turned this brilliant zealot of orthodox Judaism to a fearless Christian evangelist and apologist. Jews and the disciples alike feared him and were afraid to let him join them. "But Barnabas took him [Saul], and brought him to the apostles" (Acts 9:27). Barnabas was not intimidated by this brash convert, but drew him in and vouched for him. Undoubtedly, he encouraged and taught Saul during those early days and patiently stayed with him, knowing that time and experience would soon temper this gifted young leader.

- Barnabas illustrates a number of the specific ways that mentors help mentorees:
- Mentors give to mentorees: timely advice, resources, finances, opportunity.
- Mentors risk their own reputation in order to sponsor a mentoree.
- Mentors model various aspects of leadership functions so as to challenge mentorees to move toward them.
- Mentors direct mentorees to needed resources that will further develop them.

- Mentors co-minister with mentorees in order to increase their confidence, status, credibility, and ability.

A breakthrough comes when you see mentoring as a relational exchange between two people with varying levels of involvement and degrees of intensity.

*Intensive Mentor*
Discipler—enablement in basics of following Christ.
Spiritual Guide—accountability, direction, and insight for questions and decisions affecting spirituality.
Coach—motivation, skills, and application needed to meet a task or challenge.

*Occasional Mentor*
Counselor—timely advice and correct perspectives on viewing self, others, circumstances, and ministry.
Teacher—knowledge and understanding of a particular subject.
Sponsor—career guidance and protection as leader moves within an organization.

*Passive Mentor*
*Contemporary model*—a living personal model for life, ministry, or profession.
*Historical model*—a past life that teaches dynamic principles.

Mentoring is an empowering experience that requires a connection between two people. . .Factors such as time, proximity, needs, shared values, and goals affect any relationship. But the mentoring relationship needs three additional factors, or dynamics, to bring about empowerment.

1. Attraction—This is the necessary starting point in the mentoring relationship. The mentoree is drawn to the mentor for various reasons.
2. Responsiveness—The mentoree must be willing and ready to learn from the mentor. Attitude is crucial for the mentoree.
3. Accountability—Mutual responsibility for one another in the mentoring process ensures progress and closure.

The more deliberate and intense the mentoring relationship, the more important these dynamics are. Why is this true? Because mutual commitment is necessary for change and growth to take place. These dynamics are the ingredients that produce this commitment.

## SOLITUDE

**Objective:** The individual will demonstrate an understanding of the processes of spiritual formation through *solitude* by discussing the model of Jesus.

*Richard Foster,* Celebration of Discipline, *pp. 96, 97*

Jesus calls us from loneliness to solitude. The fear of being left alone petrifies people. A new child in the neighborhood sobs to her mother, "No one ever plays with me." A college freshman yearns for his high school days when he was the center of attention: "Now I'm a nobody." A business executive sits dejected in her office, powerful, yet alone. An old woman lies in a nursing home waiting to go "home."

Our fear of being alone drives us to noise and crowds. We keep up a constant stream of words even if they are inane. We buy radios that strap to our wrists or fit over our ears so that, if no one else is around, at least we are not condemned to silence. T. S. Elliot analyzes our culture well when he writes, "Where shall the world be found, where will the word resound? Not here, there is not enough silence."[96]

But loneliness or clatter are not our only alternatives. We can cultivate an inner solitude and silence that sets us free from loneliness and fear. Loneliness is inner emptiness. Solitude is inner fulfillment.

Solitude is more a state of mind and heart than it is a place. There is a solitude of heart that can be maintained at all times. Crowds, or the lack of them, have little to do with this inward attentiveness. It is quite possible to be a desert hermit and never experience solitude. But if we possess inward solitude, we need not fear being alone, for we know that we are not alone. Neither do we fear being with others, for they do not control us. . . . Whether alone or among people, we will always carry with us a portable sanctuary of the heart.

Inward solitude has outward manifestations. There is the freedom to be alone, not in order to be away from people, but in order to hear the divine Whisper better. Jesus lived in outward "heart solitude." He also frequently experienced outward solitude. He inaugurated His ministry by spending forty days alone in the desert (Matthew 4:1-11). Before He chose the twelve, He spent the entire night alone in the desert hills (Luke 6:12). When He received the news of John the Baptist's death, He "withdrew from there in a boat to a lonely place apart" (Matthew 14:13). After the miraculous feeding of the five thousand, Jesus "went up into the hills by himself" (Matthew 14:23). I could go on, but perhaps this is sufficient to show that the seeking out of solitary places was a regular practice for Jesus (Mark 1:35; 6:31; Luke 5:16; Matthew 17:1-9; 26:36-46). So it should be for us.

Dietrich Bonhoeffer in *Life Together* titled one of his chapters, "The Day Together," and the following chapter, "The Day Alone." Both are essential for spiritual success. He writes, "Let him who cannot be alone beware of community. . .Let him who is not in community beware of being alone. . . Each by itself has profound pitfalls and perils. One who wants fellowship without solitude plunges into the void of words and feelings, and one who seeks solitude without fellowship perishes in the abyss of vanity, self-infatuation, and despair."[97]

Therefore, we must seek out the recreating stillness of solitude if we want to be with others meaningfully. We must seek the fellowship and accountability of others if we want to be alone safely. We must cultivate both if we are to live in obedience.

There is an old proverb to the effect that "all those who open their mouths, close their eyes." The purpose of silence and solitude is to be able to see and hear. Control rather than no noise is the key to solitude. James saw clearly that the person who could control his tongue is perfect (James 3:1-12). Under the discipline of silence and solitude we learn when to speak and when to refrain from speaking. The person who views the disciplines as laws will always turn silence into an absurdity: "I'll not speak for the next forty days." This is always a severe temptation to any true disciple who wants to live under silence and solitude. Thomas A. Kempis writes, "It is easier to be silent altogether than to speak with moderation."[98] . . .There is "a time to keep silence and a time to speak" (Ecclesiastes 3:7). Control is the key.

James' analogies of the rudder and the bridle suggest to us that the tongue guides as well as controls. The tongue guides our course in many ways. If we tell a lie, we are led to telling more lies to cover up the first lie. Soon we are forced to behave in a certain way in order to give credence to the lie. No wonder James declares that "the tongue is a fire" (3:6).

The disciplined person is the person who can do what needs to be done when it needs to be done. The mark of a championship basketball team is a team that can score points when they are needed. Most of us can get the ball into the hoop eventually, but we can't do it when it is needed. Likewise, a person who is under the discipline of silence is a person who can say what needs to be said when it needs to be said. "A word fitly spoken is like apples of gold in pictures of silver" (Proverbs 25:11). If we are silent when we should speak, we are not living in the discipline of silence. If we speak when we should be silent, we again miss the mark. . . .

One reason we can hardly bear to remain silent is that it makes us feel so helpless. We are so accustomed to relying upon words to manage and control others. If we are silent, who will take control? God will take control, but we will never let Him take control until we trust Him. Silence is intimately related to trust.

The tongue is our most powerful weapon of manipulation. A frantic stream of words flows from us because we are in a constant process of adjusting our public image. We fear so deeply what we think other people see in us that we talk in order to straighten out their understanding. If I have done some wrong thing (or even some right thing that I think you may misunderstand) and discover that you know about it, I will be very tempted to help you understand my action! Silence is one of the deepest disciplines of the Spirit simply because it puts the stopper on all self-justification. One of the fruits of silence is the freedom to let God be our Justifier.

## SERVICE

**Objective:** The individual will demonstrate an understanding of the processes of spiritual formation through *service* by listing right motives for service.

*Donald S. Whitney,* Spiritual Disciplines for the Christian Life, *pp. 110-116*

Christ's summons to service is the most spiritually grand and noble way to live a life. [Yet] it is typically as pedestrian as washing someone's feet. Richard Foster puts it starkly: "In some ways we would prefer to hear Jesus' call to deny father and mother, houses and land for the sake of the gospel, than His word to wash feet. Radical self-denial gives the feel of adventure. If we forsake all, we even have the chance of glorious martyrdom. But in service we are banished to the mundane, ordinary, trivial."[99]

The ministry of serving may be as public as preaching or teaching, but more often it will be as sequestered as nursery duty. It may be as visible as singing a solo, but usually it will be as unnoticed as operating the sound equipment to amplify the solo. Serving may be as appreciated as a good testimony in a worship service, but typically it's as thankless as washing dishes after a church social. Most service, even that which seems the most glamorous, is like an iceberg. Only the eye of God ever sees the larger, hidden part of it.

That's why serving must become a spiritual discipline. The flesh connives against its hiddenness and sameness. Two of the deadliest of our sins — sloth and pride — loathe serving. They paint glazes on our eyes and put chains on our hands and feet so that we don't serve as we know we should or even as we want to. If we don't discipline ourselves to serve for the sake of Christ and His kingdom (and for the purpose of godliness), we'll serve only occasionally or when it's convenient or self-serving. The result will be a quantity and quality of service we'll regret when the day of accountability for our service comes.

In *The Spirit of the Disciplines*, Dallas Willard says, rightly, that not all serving will, or even should, be disciplined serving. However, those who want to train themselves for Christlike spirituality will find it one of the surest and most practical means of growth in grace.[100]

But lest we begin to think that serving is merely an option, let's chisel this into the cornerstone of our Christian life: *every Christian is expected to serve.* When God calls His elect to Himself, He calls no one to idleness. When we are born again and our sins forgiven, the blood of Christ cleanses our conscience according to Hebrews 9:14, in order for us to "serve the living God!" "Serve the Lord with gladness" (Psalm 100:2) is every Christian's commission. There is no such thing as spiritual unemployment or spiritual retirement in the Kingdom of God.

Of course, motive matters in the service we are to offer to God. [We are] motivated by obedience. "If two angels were to receive at the same moment a commission from God, one to go down and rule earth's grandest empire, the other to go and sweep the streets of its meanest village, it would be a matter of entire indifference to each which service fell to his lot, the post of ruler or the post of scavenger; for the joy of the angels lies only in obedience to God's will."[101]

[We are] motivated by gratitude. The Prophet Samuel exhorted the people of God to service with these words: "But be sure to fear the Lord and serve him faithfully with all your heart; consider what great things he has done for you" (1 Samuel 12:24). It is no burden to serve God when we consider what great things He has done for us.

He has never done anything greater for anyone, nor could He do anything greater for you, than bring you to Himself. Suppose He put ten million dollars in your bank account every morning for the rest of your life, but He didn't save you? Suppose He gave you the most beautiful face and body of anyone who ever lived, a body that never aged for a thousand years, but then at death He shut you out of heaven and into hell for eternity? What has God ever given anyone that could compare with the salvation He has given to us as believers? . . . If we cannot be grateful servants of Him who is everything and in whom we have everything, what will make us grateful?

[We are] motivated by gladness. The inspired command of Psalms 100:2 is, "Serve the Lord with gladness." We are not to serve God grudgingly or grimly, but gladly. In the courts of ancient kings, servants were often executed for nothing more than looking sad in the service of the king. Nehemiah, in chapter two, verse two of the book that bears his name, was grieving over the news he'd heard that Jerusalem was still in ruins despite the return of many Jews from the Babylonian exile. As he was serving food to King Artaxerxes one day, the king said to him, "Why does your face look so sad when you are not ill? This can be nothing but sadness of heart." Because of what that could mean for him, Nehemiah writes, "I was very much afraid." You don't mope or sulk when you serve a king. Not only does it give the appearance that you don't want to serve the king, but it is a statement of dissatisfaction with the way he's running things. Something is wrong if you can't serve the Lord with gladness.

[We are] motivated by forgiveness, not guilt.

The heir of heaven serves his Lord simply out of gratitude; he has no salvation to gain, no heaven to lose . . . now, out of love to the God who chose him, and who gave so great a price for his redemption, he desires to lay himself out entirely to his Master's service. O you who are seeking salvation by the works of the law, what a miserable life your's must be!. . .The child of God works not for life, but from life; he does not work to be saved, he works because he is saved.[102]

# ENDNOTES

[1]Dallas Willard, *Spirit of the Disciplines* (San Francisco: Harper Collins Publishers, 1988), p. 239

[2]*Ibid.*, p. 70

[3]Francis de Sales, *Introduction to the Devout Life* (Garden City, NY: Doubleday, Image Books, 1957), pp. 43, 44.

[4]Dallas Willard, *In Search of Guidance* (New York: Harper and Collins, 1993), p. 12.

[5]Thomas H. Groome, *Christian Religious Education: Sharing Our Story and Vision* (San Francisco: Harper & Row, 1980), p. 141.

[6]Francis Frangipane, *Holiness, Truth, and the Presence of God* (Cedar Rapids: IA: Advancing Church Publications, 1986), p. 79.

[7]George Barna, *What Americans Believe* (Ventura, CA: Regal Books, 1991), p. 155.

[8]James Strong, *Strong's Exhaustive Concordance of the Bible* (Nashville: Regal, n.d.).

[9]R. Kent Hughes, *Disciplines of a Godly Man* (Wheaton, IL: Crossway Books, 1991), p. 14.

[10]Elton Trueblood, quoted in *Leadership,* Summer, 1989, 10(3): p. 60.

[11]Barclay, *op. cit.,* I:284.

[12]Richard Foster, *Celebration of Discipline* (San Francisco: Harper & Row, 1978), p. 8.

[13]Willard, *op. cit.,* p. 146.

[14]Henri Nouwen, *Making All Things New* (San Francisco: Harper Collins, 1981), pp. 49, 50.

[15]Strong, *op. cit.*

[16]Martin Luther quoted by Harry Emerson Fosdick, ed., *Great Voices of the Reformation* (New York: Modern Library, 1954), pp. 121, 122.

[17]Walter Marshall quoted by A. W. Pink, *The Doctrine of Sanctification* (Swengel, PA: Bible Truth Depot, 1955), p. 29.

[18]Shelley, *op. cit.*

[19]William M. Greathouse, *From the Apostles to Wesley: Christian Perfection in Historical Perspective* (Grand Rapids: Eerdmans, 1979), pp. 96, 97.

[20]David Watson, *I Believe in the Church* (London: Holder and Stoughton, 1978), p. 23.

[21]Barna, *op. cit.*

[22]Francis Schaeffer, *True Spirituality* (Wheaton, IL: Tyndale, 1984), p. 17.

[23]Schaff; Creeds; *op. cit.*

[24]Edmund Jacob, *Theology of the Old Testament* (New York: Harper & Bros., 1958), p. 86.

[25]Norman H. Snaith, *The Distinctive Ideas of the Old Testament* (London: Epworth, 1960), p. 43.

[26]Greathouse, *op. cit.*, p. 19.

[27]Gustaf Aulen, *The Faith of the Christian Church* (Philadelphia: Fortress, 1960), p. 132.

[28]Greathouse, *op. cit.*, pp. 20, 21.

[29]Jacob, *op. cit.*, p. 88.

[30]Emil Brunner, *The Christian Doctrine of God* (London: Lutterworth, 1960), p. 159.

[31]Snaith, *op. cit.*, p. 47.

[32]Alfred Edersheim, *Bible History: Old Testament* (Grand Rapids: Eerdmans, 1949), 2:110.

[33]Walter Eichrodt, *Theology of the Old Testament* (Philadelphia: Westminster, 1961), I:137.

[34]George Allen Turner, *The Vision Which Transforms* (Kansas City: Beacon Hill, 1964), p. 41.

[35]Greathouse, *op. cit.*, p. 23.

[36]*Ibid.*, p. 24.

[37]*Ibid.*

[38]Foster, *op. cit.*, p. 163.

[39]Fosef Goldbrunner, quoted in Willard, *Disciplines, op. cit.*, p. 75.

[40]Michel Quoist, *The Christian Response* (Wheaton, IL: Crossway, 1993), p. 21.

[41]Strong's *Concordance, op. cit.*

[42]Willard, *Disciplines, op. cit.*, p. 86.

[43]Jonathan Edwards quoted in Jerry Bridges, *Pursuit of Holiness* (Colorado Springs: NavPress, 1978), p. 96.

[44]Jerry Bridges, *Ibid.*

[45]Francis Frangipane, *The Three Battlegrounds* (Cedar Rapids, IA: Morningstar, 1989), p. v.

[46]*Ibid.*, p. 9.

[47]Roberta Bondi, *To Love As God Loves* (Philadelphia: Fortress, 1987), p. 55.

[48]*Ibid.*, p. 54.

[49]Watchman Nee, *The Release of the Spirit* (Cloverdale, IN: Ministry of Life, 1965), p. 12.

[50]Willard, *op. cit.,* p. 16.

[51]Strong's Concordance, *op. cit.,* The Greek *skenoo* means "to tent or encamp, to occupy, or to reside (as God did in the tabernacle of old, a symbol of protection and communion): dwell."

[52]Willard, *op. cit.,* p. 74.

[53]James Jean quoted in Willard, *op. cit.*

[54]Greathouse, *op. cit.,* pp. 16, 17.

[55]Michael Green, *Evangelism in the Early Church* (Grand Rapids: Eerdmans , 1970), p. 275.

[56]Jim Peterson, *Living Proof* (Colorado Springs: NavPress, 1989), p. 73; *Pentecostal Explosion,* Synan, *op. cit.*

[57]Robert E. Coleman, *Nothing To Do But To Save Souls* (Grand Rapids: Francis Asbury, 1990) p. 18- 20.

[58]Millard J. Erickson, ed., "Toward a Biblical Doctrine of the Church," *The New Life: Readings in Christian Theology* (Grand Rapids: Baker, 1972), p. 272.

[59]Howard Belben, *The Mission of Jesus* (Colorado Springs: NavPress, 1985), p. 69.

[60]If we consider Paul the first generation, Timothy would have been the second generation. Of course, there were others with him such as Titus, Luke, John Mark, and so on. The third generation would be the faithful men that these men gathered around them and worked with to pour into from God's work in their lives. The fourth generation would be seen in these faithful men working with others, pouring from their lives as well. This multiplying strategy of discipleship has been used by the commercial world in the last few decades. The principle works whether it is used for the

growth of the church or for the growth of commerce. The regrettable fact is that the leaders of industry have utilized this principle clearly modeled by Jesus and Paul while the Christian world has failed to use the power of this New Testament example of discipleship.

[61]D. James Kennedy, *Evangelism Explosion* (Wheaton: Tyndale, 1983), p. 4. Used by permission.

[62]Shelley, *op. cit.*, p. 42.

[63]Kennedy, *op. cit.*, p. 4

[64]The word "equip" does not appear in the KJV Bible. The Greek verb is *katartizo*, "to furnish completely." It is translated "perfecting" in the KJV, but "equip" in Weymouth, Montgomery, Phillips, The New English Bible, NASB, and RSV.

[65]University of Tennessee at Chattanooga, inscription on the marble wall of the small campus prayer chapel

[66]George Barna, *How To Find Your Church* (Minneapolis: Worldwide, 1989), p. 93.

[67]Win Arn, *The Church Growth Ratio Book* (Pasadena, CA: Church Growth, 1987), p. 10.

[68]C. Peter Wagner, Win Arn, and Elmer Towns, ed., *Church Growth: State of the Art* (Wheaton, IL: Tyndale, 1986).

[69]*Sharing Eternal Life Trainer's Manual* (Cleveland, TN: White Wing).

[70]Kennedy, *op. cit.*, p. 3.

[71]James D. Simpson, *Uncover Your Spiritual Gifts* (Cleveland, TN: Pentecostal Institute of Church Growth, 1988).

[72]Watson, *op. cit.*, p. 18.

[73]Joseph Tosini, *Is There Not A Cause?* ( Columbus, OH: Cityhill, 1989), p. 226

[74]Jim Peterson, *Church Without Walls* (Colorado Springs: NavPress, 1992), p. 203.

[75]Shelley, *op. cit.*, p. 49.

[76]Gerhard Lohfink, *Jesus and Community: the Social Dimension of Christian Faith*, John P. Galvin (Philadelphia: Fortress, 1984), pp. 104-106.

[77]Francis Schaeffer, *The Church at the End of the Twentieth Century* (Westchester, IL: Crossway, 1970), p. 63.

[78]Tosini, *op. cit.*, pp. 56, 58, 65, 66. See also David Matthew, "God Wants a Family," *Church Adrift* (United Kingdom: Marshall, Morgan, and Scott, 1985), p. 25.

[79]Kenneth Hagin, *New Thresholds of Faith* (Tulsa: Rhema, 1980), p. 7.

[80]Smith Wigglesworth as quoted by Kenneth Hagin, *op. cit.*,p. 23. See Stanley Howard Frodsham, *Smith Wigglesworth: Apostle of Faith*, (Springfield, MO: Gospel, 1948).

[81]E. M. Bounds, *Power Through Prayer* (Chicago: Moody, n.d.), p. 23. This is an excellent reading on prayer. See also Richard Foster, *Prayer, Finding the Heart's True Home* (San Francisco: Harper, 1992).

[82]Foster, *Discipline, op. cit.*, p. 38.

[83]*Ibid.*, pp. 38, 77.

[84]*Ibid.*, pp. 41, 54.

[85]*Ibid.*, p. 13.

[86]*Ibid.*, p. 36, 37.

[87]*Ibid.*, p. 45.

[88]Thomas R. Kelly, *A Testament of Devotion* (New York: Harper, 1941), p. 128.

[89]Foster, *op. cit.*, p. 49.

[90]Foster, *op. cit.*, pp. 64, 65.

[91]*Ibid.*, p. 67.

[92]Donald Bloesch, quoted in Whitney, *op. cit.*, p. 195.

[93]"Are We Becoming Reformed Men?" *The Banner of Truth*, March, 1991, p. 5.

[94]Edmund S. Morgan, *The Puritan Family* (New York: Harper & Row, 1966), p. 5.

[95]Whitney, *op. cit.*, p. 197.

[96]Elizabeth O'Conner, *Search for Silence* (Waco, TX: Word, 1971), p. 132.

[97]Dietrich Bonhoeffer, *Life Together* (New York: Harper & Row, 1952), pp. 77, 78.

[98]Thomas A. Kempis, *The Imitation of Christ* (New York: Pyramid, 1967), p. 18.

[99]Foster, *Discipline, op. cit.*, p. 110.

[100]Willard, *Disciplines, op. cit.*, p. 182.

[101]E. M. Bounds, *The Essentials of Prayer* (Grand Rapids: Baker, 1979), p. 19.

[102]"Serving the Lord With Gladness," in *The Metropolitan Tabernacle Pulpit* (Pasadena, TX: Pilgrim, 1989), XIII: 495, 496.

# FOUNDATIONS COURSE: Spiritual Formation

## Registration Form for: Ministers, Ministerial Candidates and Certified Teacher Candidates

Name: _____

Address: _____

_____

Local Church: _____

Pastor: _____

In order to earn a Certificate of Completion or Leadership Development Unit the ministerial candidate should register with the state/regional/national office. The following criteria must be met:

- The ministerial candidate must be approved by the Overseer.
- The ministerial participant must complete the course of study in a reasonable time.
- The approved CBL text must be read and the accompanying examination and assignments successfully completed with a score of 90% (open-book test). The Examination should be sent to the state/regional/ national office for grading.

I am a candidate for:

❒ Minister's License      ❒ Minister Upgrading
❒ Certified Teacher       ❒ Individual Study

Please indicate which of the following you are requesting credit for:

❒ LDU Credit
❒ Leadership Certificate
❒ Advanced Leadership Certificate
❒ State/Regional Credit
❒ Individual Study

Date _____      Grade _____

Applicant Signature: _____